Church

One Pilgrim's Progress

Church

One Pilgrim's Progress

David Johnson Rowe

ISBN 978-1-329-69525-2

Proceeds from this book are given to the work of FOCI (Friends of Christ in India). For more information, visit the website at www.foci.org.

Dedication

To Emma

To all who love and reach

To life's mystery, sorrow and joy

To love's wonders

To heaven's surprises

To Church

Contents

Acknowledgements

Alida's partnership in life, ministry and marriage extends to my books. A patient listener, an ardent supporter, and a wise editor, she has a far better story to tell than I.

Rachel Baumann and Sarah Milicia provided keen eyes, fresh perspectives, and youthful sensitivities while reading and typing the various illegible manuscripts I handed them. Kirsten Navin's cover art captures the beauty and simplicity of our church as a symbol of Church at its best. Roni Widmer kept chaos away from my piles of paper and from daily life.

The people of Greenfield Hill Congregational Church have always been encouraging, giving me time away to write in coffeehouses from Fairfield to New Haven to the Berkshires to Prague. Here's the proof that I wasn't just overindulging in cappuccino all that time. Speaking of which: I thank all the baristas in all those coffeehouses, whose friendliness, humor, coffee and even faith made every day of writing a pleasure.

I offer humble gratitude to several friends whose generosity brought this book into print. Thank you for believing.

Lastly, thank you to every church which ever let me in the front door. I learned from every one.

Notes

Most often, I have capitalized 'Church' when it represents Church as an idea, an ideal: church at its best.

Scripture quotations are taken primarily from the New International Version (NIV). In places, I drew from my memories of the King James Version (KJV). In some cases, I offered my own paraphrasing.

Foreword

Ivan Klima writes, in *Love and Garbage,* "there are nearly five thousand million people living in the world and every one of them believes that his life is good for at least one story." This is mine. Unfortunately, Klima goes on to say that if some master hand were to erase all the redundancies from all those stories, "scarcely a sentence would be left." Well, let the master hand reach for the eraser as I tell my story. This is the story of Church as I have lived it, as I have loved it, and as it has loved me back.

ONE

The Worst Day of My Life

It was late afternoon, I was in my living room, when I heard the worst scream of my life coming from outside. I knew it was Alida, I knew it was something earth-shattering, and as I looked out the window I saw her stumbling across the village green to the house. I met her at the door, where she collapsed in grief. "Emma, she's killed herself."

As co-pastors, as husband and wife, Alida and I are called on to minister to others in every possible circumstance ... but there are times when we are as devastated as everyone around us. Emma was a true bright light in our personal life, in our family life, in our church life. We had known her forever, the forever of her sixteen years. Since her death I have learned more about suicide than I knew there was to know. I know even less now.

What I knew at that moment was that Emma was an amazing, vibrant, delightful, faithful young woman. She was wonderfully talented, full of life, with a deeply loving family, and surrounded by friends. These thoughts flooded my head as we picked ourselves up off the floor, got in the car and drove the short distance to Emma's home. In those few minutes we resolved that we would not let anyone sully her name or hurt her family. All too often at such times people become amateur psychologists and instant experts, all too ready with half-baked explanations, pet theories and lousy theology. For something we cannot explain.

The short drive to Emma's was the longest of our lives, and the sorrow we met was the deepest of our lives. I would have told you that my extensive pastoral career had prepared me for anything. I would have been wrong.

Walking through the front door we heard sobs that came from a place only a few can know. All the euphemisms for sorrow are so true: grief-stricken, heart-broken, sorrow-ful. Life, dreams, family, plans: all shattered. In our embraces with Emma's parents it felt like taking all the hurts of the universe in our arms.

The deaths of my life have taught me to make an important request. I asked Emma's folks if I could go to Emma. It was my way of saying she still is, she still matters, she is loved, all in the present tense. They seemed to welcome it, and the police were kind and understanding.

I went into her room and found Emma. I took her in my arms, I talked with her, I prayed with her, I made her some promises.

Such sorrow requires a lot of waiting while various officials ask unanswerable questions. Police, medical examiner, psychologist, family, neighbors, all of our collective wisdom truly was "full of sound and fury, signifying nothing." Nothing. But we tried.

Perhaps Jesus' most audacious statement is the beatitude, "blessed are they that mourn" (Matthew 5:4). That's the part of the verse everyone knows, and even that much seems crass. Modern translations say that Jesus meant, "How happy are those that mourn." That evening, in Emma's house, Jesus' statement felt cruel. And Jesus' follow-up phrase, "for they shall be comforted," seemed flat out impossible.

However, some folks don't want to give up on Jesus, especially in the worst of times. If religion is a crutch and the opiate of the masses (as Freud and Marx liked to say) then pass the opium and hand me a crutch. If Jesus had a thought to get us through this horror I needed to know it. In that moment I truly needed to remember something Tony Campolo said. He was an old friend from my Habitat for Humanity days, and his take on Jesus' beatitude stuck with me for its boldness. Tony heard Jesus saying, "Blessed are those whose hearts are broken by that which breaks the heart of God." Blessed are those who weep for what makes God weep. In other words, God was in Emma's house with us, and it was just as bad for God as for us. The one thing I knew for certain was that God's heart was broken, God was weeping. I was strangely comforted. Later that night Alida and I and Emma's parents went again to be with Emma.

If the true meaning of the Cross is that love conquers death then in Emma's room that triumph began. It was love that made the sorrow so great. It was love that would take us beyond the sorrow. There was so much love, unending I truly believe, and so much hurt, just as unending on this side of heaven. On the other side love wins.

On this side it can feel like a draw at best. Blessedly, Emma's family was the best. Thus ended the worst day of my life.

The Best Day of My Life

Church.

An odd word to bridge the worst to best, but Church was our bridge. Church as building, but more than building. Church as faith, but more than faith. Church as people, but as more than people. Church as idea, as place, as tradition, as family. Yet more like Church as organizing principle. That seems such a cold phrase in the middle of this story, but it is descriptive. To realize all of our hopes for honoring Emma's life we organized the memorial service around the principle of Church. Church, itself, is organized around the principle of Good News. Could our Good News sustain us all from the worst day of life to the best? That was our challenge. We say so. We preach, teach and sing so. Our scriptures tell us so.

The jaunty Easter hymn proclaims, "Up from the grave he arose!" The 23rd Psalm promises, "Yea though I walk through the Valley of the Shadow of Death I will fear no evil... and I shall dwell in the house of the Lord forever." Jesus said to the so-called good thief crucified alongside him, "thou shalt be with me in Paradise" (Luke 23:43). St. Paul, having met the resurrected Jesus, boldly declares, "In a moment, in the twinkling of an eye, the dead shall be raised incorruptible!" (1 Corinthians 15:52). That's our Church DNA telling us so. Could we live it just as convincingly?

The challenge was immediate. Neighbors filled the street outside. There was, literally, a whole town to tell. Emma lived a full life, and she was at the height of that life. Fully engaged in high school, church, jazz band, chorus, youth group, summer camp, there was a whole world about to begin their own part of our worst day. In short order there was anger, grief, guilt, fear, gossip, confusion, concern, regrets. All of that was very real.

Just as real were laughter, love, memories, stories, photos, and her trademark fedoras. There was a life to be honored and an eternal life to be assured, and Church was at the heart of it.

Our goal was simple: with Church as a foundation we would build a celebration of a wonderful girl from a wonderful family who had lived a life full of wonder. The mystery of her death would not define her life nor deny the miracle of her life.

The next night two hundred teenagers crammed into our Len Morgan Youth Barn for a powerful night that would test everything we held dear from the hardest to the holiest. Contradictions and paradoxes were everywhere, not just in the mix of tears and laughter. Alida, whose pastoral ministry with teenagers is legendary, instinctively knew the complexities of that night. The range from freshmen to seniors, from celebration to guilt, from faith to anger, from remembrance to fear, was fully felt in the Barn. We also knew that we had to do both suicide prevention and remove the stigma of suicide. My fear was that everyone there was as fragile as I was.

Here's the truth. That night our young people embodied Church. They were pastor, preacher, Father Confessor, priest, all rolled into Church as a living thing. They were healer, prophet, and teacher. They were Holy Communion. They were the Last Supper, the Crucifixion and the Resurrection.

During the final days of Jesus' life he experienced community, humiliation, fear, betrayal, tears, denial, agony, forgiveness, emptiness, doubt, faith, and then the euphoria of love. We did it in two hours, but it was just the beginning.

The actual funeral is neither the beginning nor the end, but it is a very real way station. The death of every loved one divides our time into before and after. Before, when they were alive. After, when they are not. The funeral becomes the last stop as we transfer permanently from before to after.

When Church is done right we celebrate before and after. And with Emma we did Church right. With Emma's high school jazz band, with Emma's community chorus, with Emma's mom and dad and sister, with Emma's school friends and Church family we answered the age-old Biblical question, "is there a balm in Gilead?" (Jeremiah 8:22) Together, we immersed ourselves in the meaning and delight of her life and felt the mystical balm of God's love at work. Faith, family and friends were the balm. Our church was Gilead. It turns out that there is a balm in Gilead.

Part of what worked for me was an image that struck both Alida and me immediately that week. When Emma breathed her last we imagined her taken immediately to heaven where she was met just as immediately by our church's Len Morgan. Not by St. Peter, not by other relatives, not by some heavenly inquisition. It was Len Morgan, gently but persistently pushing his way through the crowd to be the first to greet her.

Who was Len Morgan? Len was a legendary elderly gentleman who served our Church in a million ways but preferred to be known as our Church's "oldest teenager." His love for our young people was absolutely Godly. In other words, unconditional. That's a big word, unconditional. We may believe in it, we may aim for it. But I know that I have a tendency to pile up conditions for every affection. Performance standards, hoops to jump through, sins to avoid. Meet my expectations, and I will love you. That's me, not Len Morgan.

Len worked with our church youth for twenty years at weekly meetings and our annual mission trips to Appalachia, countless days with countless kids. He had a perfect record. In all that time Len never met a bad kid, never gave up on one. Every kid was just right. So on earth we were all stricken and broken by Emma's death, torturing ourselves with questions about "why" and regrets about "shoulda, coulda, woulda." But in heaven Len pushes his way past St. Peter at the Pearly Gates, past anyone with a question or a recrimination or so much as a "tsk, tsk." And I see him speed up to be sure that Emma sees him first. Because Len knows. Whatever doubts she had, or regrets, or fears so carefully hidden, must have seemed overwhelming. Which is why Len had to be there first. Because heaven is not a place for fear. So, with a little shake of his head and his great Alabama twinkle, he hugs her, and Emma melts into the hug.

I confess, that image got me through the week. Hour by hour I was carried along by an extraordinary array of people, events, kindnesses and thoughts that, in the words of an old hymn, "planted my feet on higher ground."[1]

---

[1] *I'm pressing on the upward way.* Johnson Oatman, Jr. (1856-1922). Written in 1898 and published in *Songs of Love and Praise, No 5* (Philadelphia,1898)

On that higher ground we had a funeral service that enabled folks in the depths of sorrow to experience the view from up there as truly spectacular. Led by her parents, Peter and Nancy, by her amazing sister, Sarah, led by a church filled with her friends, led by a remarkable life and an indomitable faith, we linked heaven and earth in a tangible way. When we left Church there was resilience to her life. Inspired by Peter and Nancy, many have worked to help our church youth and school system and wider community bring suicide prevention to the heart of our mission. The life of Emma in our hearts keeps others alive.

I have taken a whole chapter to tell one story to make a simple point. Church was the bridge from the worst day of my life to the best. Part of the miracle within sorrow is that when Church is done right God is incredibly real, scripture is incredibly true, Church is incredibly alive. When that happens on the worst day you know you are in the right place.

It is true that I experienced and understood this image of heaven in a literal, human, personal, intimate way – and this would make some of my favorite seminary professors uncomfortable. I do humanize heaven and "anthropomorphize" God by envisioning God as a sentient being who would willingly step aside to allow Len to hug Emma first. Anthropomorphism is seeing God in human terms. It is what leads to sentiments like "put yourself in God's hands" ... "God's eye is on the sparrow" ... "our father who art in heaven" ... "He walks with me and talks with me." I plead guilty to it.

Since God seems to have anthropomorphized God's self by becoming Jesus, I am quite willing to see God in human terms. During the Christmas season we embrace anthropomorphism. An angel told Mary that the baby Jesus would be "Emmanuel, which means God with us" (Matthew 1:23). John's more theological Christmas story tells us "the word became flesh" (John 1:14). Basic Christian teaching is that in the thirty-three year life of Jesus on earth God was here with arms and legs and ears and mouth.

It has been said by a greater mind than mine that if you have a hard time grasping the concept of God, don't worry, focus on Jesus. Jesus is "the near end of God."[2] Jesus is God made understandable for those of us who need a little help. So I don't have a problem imagining a very real Len Morgan embracing a very real Emma with a very real hug, washing away very real tears and sorrows, and then turning to really walk hand in hand into a very real heaven.

If Jesus is the near end of God, Church is the near end of Jesus. We exist to turn the worst days into best days. We exist to bridge before and after. We exist to make now better.

---

[2] Attributed to a sermon preached by Harry Emerson Fosdick

Two

The Family Business and My Coney Island Conversion

My earliest memory is of sleeping on the back pew of my father's Advent Christian Church in Lynn, Massachusetts during an evening service. It is a warm and pleasant and comfortable memory, a fitting first memory for a life lived mostly in Church. Church has been my life, career, calling, fun, job, family and home.

As a preacher and pastor I have emphasized the idea of "church family", and that is exactly how I have experienced it. When I was kicked out of college it was the welcoming and unconditional love of my childhood church family that spurred me toward conversion, salvation, and a lifetime in ministry. That my church family could so easily mirror the best attributes of my real family made the concept of church family central to my ministry.

The Church Universal has also proven to be home and family. Wherever my mission travels have taken me, someone someplace, church connected, was always there to make me feel at home. In war-torn Uganda, a Catholic priest, Father Egidio, took me in, pumped me up, kept me going. Pentecostal street preachers in Kenya, Base Community theological revolutionaries in Nicaragua, indigenous church Kimbanguists in the Congo, Mother Teresa's folks in Calcutta, high church Anglicans in Edinburgh, Bishops and lay catechists and Gideons and missionaries anywhere and everywhere proved the promise of The Church Universal: that wherever you go there is a church family waiting to embrace you.

Church has literally been my home, my community, my playground. For all but three years of my life I have lived in parsonages, usually within the shadow of the steeple.

My first kiss was in church, my first date and first dance. As a kid I hit batting practice in the Sunday School Assembly Hall. As an adult I had my Babe Ruth League baseball team practice pitching in the sanctuary and fielding in Fellowship Hall. It was the way I was raised, and the way I lived. The best meals, best friends, best memories, best hopes are all church flavored.

Church is also the family business. For over a hundred years and into four generations, Church has been at the center of our lives.

My father preached his first sermon at the age of twelve and retired seventy-five years later. My grandfather, with a fourth grade education, kept preaching and teaching and caring into his early eighties. Uncle Gerald and Uncle Lloyd lived out their lives in pastoral ministry. Cousins, sisters and brothers in law served in the mission field.

Church life, church ministry, pastoral work, that is our family business, and not just for the ordained male clergy on the family tree. Spouses and children and cousins who might never describe themselves as being "in ministry" have served as Sunday School Superintendents and teachers, Vacation Bible School leaders, church musicians and choir directors, youth workers and summer camp staff. My children have given decades of priceless service to our ministry in India without any title or pay or status that denotes clergy. Yet they serve. It is our second nature, maybe our first for that matter.

One summer for a family reunion we all gathered at my Uncle Gerald's church in Middlebury, Vermont. We pitched in as janitors to help clean the sanctuary on Saturday. At church on Sunday, Aunt Persis played the organ, my mother joined my Aunts Josephine and Madeline in a Gospel trio, Uncle Gerald played the trumpet, Uncle Lloyd and my father led worship. Church as family, family as church. It is our way of life. What my grandfather began in the early 20th century, Alida and I now take into the heart of the 21st. The family business.

It is not the kind of business you inherit; it is not passed on from generation to generation. In fact, I cannot remember a single conversation with my father that even hinted at my becoming a pastor. First and foremost, it is a calling. We entered ministry at a time when we were expected to articulate our sense of call, our certainty that God's anthropomorphic hand had been placed sturdily upon our shoulder and that God had spoken as clearly to us as to Isaiah, asking, "Whom shall I send? Who will go for us?" (Isaiah 6:8). It was expected that our "call" should be as firmly felt as when Jesus said to Peter, Andrew, James, and John, "follow me and I will make you fishers of men" (Matthew 4:18-19).

One by one we said "yes." Our church ministries have run the gamut. Grandpa Rowe's pastoral career was almost entirely the old-fashioned, St. Paul-like "tentmaker ministry". That means you work a secular job to pay the bills, and do church work in your spare time. Grandpa was a master carpenter and a paper mill foreman while serving churches from Maine to Florida. At one church he physically built it with his hands during the week and spiritually on the weekend. My father had a classic, post-World War II church career. He progressed from tiny rural New England churches to a large urban church in Brooklyn. Along the way he made Church, which was at the center of his life, into the center of the community and neighborhood surrounding it.

When I wrote *Faith at Work*, my theology of work, I reflected on my father's example:

11

One of the reasons I became a pastor was because I admired the potential for a fully integrated work-life. My model was my father. While growing up, I went visiting with him in homes, jails, hospitals, nursing homes, and funeral homes. He coached my baseball teams, and when there was no league for boys in the area, he started one. During a subway strike he drove people to their work. He played handball with the rabbi, and together they tackled community issues. He lit the community Christmas tree, delivered food baskets to the poor, met with the mayor, marched with Martin Luther King Jr., performed marriage ceremonies, and blessed the children. In the summer we went to the Catskill Mountains, where my father was a Boy Scout chaplain. That was vacation! He did it all. I had no idea where his paid pastoral work started or ended. All of it was his life's work.[3]

I followed that model, updated for my generation. Fortunately, I have always served exceptional churches in which the people delighted in an extraordinary definition of pastoral ministry. I have coached high school wrestlers, organized walks for the hungry, hosted radio shows on "religion and rock 'n' roll" and "religion in the news," wrote books, spoke all over the United States, led work camps overseas, coached YMCA basketball and Babe Ruth baseball, held teen-age dances, sponsored plays and musicals and movies, formed a track team for little kids, scrubbed pots at a soup kitchen, led worship and taught classes for the elderly at Senior Centers and nursing homes. The churches I have served have understood

---

[3] Rowe, David Johnson. *Faith at Work*. Smyth and Helwys, 1994. 5

that all of this was part of pastoral ministry. From generation to generation, each pastor in our family has found those activities that engaged him or her with their congregation and community.

But the heart of church ministry remains the same. My father taught me that the bases had to be covered, always: good preaching, useful teaching and diligent pastoral care. Without those in place, no church would be happy to hear that you've spent the afternoon coaching baseball.

My career path was a classic one. After a few youth pastor jobs in seminary and a brief stint as an Associate Pastor, I was itching to lead my own church. I was from the generation that thought we were going to save Church from irrelevance, and I was anxious to prove it. I took that vanity to a string of rural, urban, suburban churches across four denominations, enjoying four year and seven year pastorates before experiencing the surprising joy of a long-term stay. Happily, I have never lost the sense of Church as family or home, and as a place of great adventure.

My father's church career laid the foundation for my church career. My grandfather's faith laid the foundation for my faith.

Most of what I know of my grandfather's ministry comes from stories I heard. But three stories I experienced first-hand shaped me immeasurably.

When I was five my father and I took the bus from Bangor, Maine, to Florida to visit my grandparents. This was before Disney World. Instead of The Magic Kingdom, they took me to a mobile trailer "death row" complete with jail cell and an electric chair. My grandfather, passionate about pacifism since the moment of his conversion, wanted to make an impact on my thinking. It worked. I sat in the chair. That was the beginning of my life-long opposition to the death penalty.

When I was seven we visited them at their next church in upstate New York. One morning Grandpa and I were playing catch, a rite of passage in those days. After a few minutes he excused himself, went down into the basement, and re-emerged with a full set of catcher's equipment, glove, shin guards, chest protector, mask. Musty, moldy, probably thirty years old and three times too big, but once he put "the tools of ignorance" on me, I was hooked for life. For the next fourteen years I was a catcher, from Little League to college.

When I was nineteen he marked me for life, in a good way. My teenage years were already marked, but in a bad way. From street gangs to being kicked out of prep school, I reached bottom when I was kicked out of college. Skipping the salacious details, it is enough to say that I was not a nice person. You would not have wanted to know me, date me, employ me or live next to me. Even the Army didn't want me. My mess of a life only added to the long, hot summer of 1966 that the whole nation was experiencing. I can only imagine the hushed conversations in the kitchen, about me, among my parents and grandparents.

What marked me forever was my grandfather's approach. We were in the living room, and he was seated in a large chair. He asked me to come over to him, so I sort of knelt beside him. Grandpa put his hand on my head and began to pray. He asked God to touch me, use me, call me, save me. No shouting. No recrimination. No threatening. No guilt. Just two people who seemed on pretty good terms, God and my grandfather, talking about a mutual concern. Me.

It was time for a change. My grandfather knew it. My parents knew it. My roommates knew it. My college knew it. Even I was starting to know it.

Change, in religious terms, is called "conversion." The very word stirs controversy when people remember the forced

conversion of African slaves, the mass conversions often or-
chestrated by a tribal leader, or "rice conversions" done for
personal gain or survival. We imagine conversion being the
result of manipulation, pressure, inducement, guilt, fear.

While not entirely true, such skepticism is warranted. Several times I have taken youth groups to rallies and tournaments and events that included "altar calls" fueled by threatening and overwrought rhetoric meant to induce fear and
guilt. At one service Jerry Falwell, disappointed in the meagre
response to his message, pointed directly at our group up in
the balcony, telling people to reach out to my youth group and
bring them down front. On another occasion a star college
basketball player tried to frighten our youth into conversion
with tragic stories of other youth who had been killed in acci-
dents before being saved, and were now in hell.

When Billy Graham produced films for mass distribution
in theaters, I attended a workshop for local pastors. They
wanted us to seed the audience with Church members. Then,
when the movie ended with Dr. Graham's invitation to come
forward and accept Christ, Christians would get up and go
down the aisle, sort of giving courage or cover to others who
might be shy or hesitant.

But behind such clever ruse or outright manipulation is an
earnest desire to truly save a person's soul, to give that person
eternal life and the joys of heaven. Let's face it, some folks
need to change, and I, for one, needed a major overhaul. I had
lost my way. Here I was, the son and grandson of pastors,
blessed with the best of spiritual opportunities. I went to a
prep school founded by legendary evangelist, D.L. Moody, and
a college founded by thirteen Baptist pastors. And still I had
lost my way. I had a religious pedigree equal to St. Paul's yet it
turns out we both needed our own "Damascus Road" conversion. We both needed to be startled by God. For Paul, he was
literally on the road to Damascus (Acts 9:3-6) where he was

15

headed to do everything in his power to destroy Christianity. To his utter amazement, the risen Christ called him out, struck him down, and left him to think for a while. Paul decided to convert, to change, to become a new person. That's how he became Saint Paul.

My "Damascus Road" experience took place on the Coney Island Boardwalk in Brooklyn. I had been resolutely dissolute for too long. Selfish. Wasted, in the fullest sense of the word. In classic Christian terms I was a sinner. To sin is to miss the mark. God sets a target and when you miss it that is a sin. The word is so overused it has lost its power, and it is supposed to have power. When you realize how real your sin is, that is powerful. At last, I was starting to realize it.

On a plane ride to India, I read an excellent memoir of faith, *Miles to Cross,* by Mike Howerton. Reading his conversion story was startling: Howerton's description of his pre-conversion life could have been a depiction of my own life before conversion. It was not just startling, it was troubling, because I wouldn't have wanted to know the person he described. But as disconcertingly accurate as his depiction of the ugliness was, just as accurate was his description of conversion, that point at which God "invaded (his) material existence." Howerton writes:

> Jesus embraced me. My concept of sin was still being formed and I woke up late on a Sunday afternoon sick with it. My soul was filthy. What festered was the whisper that I had lived here before, that I had always lived here, that this sickness wasn't passing, that it was unto death. I felt hopeless. Life was hopeless. I was weary with the knowledge that I could not change my life. I was haunted by this: if I could have changed, I would have changed already. Instead, I floundered in a mire of my own creating. I took a walk on Little Dume with my dog. The beach was deserted, the sky spit rain, Novem-

ber. I remember looking out at the kelp forest swaying in the bay. It looked so peaceful, so appealing. The chaos and guilt and paranoia that was my life longed for the gentle sleep that the water promised. "Swim out, swim down," the siren song played, "we'll hold you, we'll help you." In this moment of life without hope or future, these were the voices that urged my destruction. Instead, I looked up. I could see the raindrops falling from a great height. I spoke out loud to the sky, to myself, to the God who turned out to be nearer than myself, and I said, "If you are real, and if you want me, then now would be a good time to tell me." It was a prayer heaved skyward from the edge of a cliff. And then Jesus embraced me. I wish it was a Spielberg moment, clouds swirling, becoming celestial arms, a voice thundering from the heavens, sand-crabs joining the dolphins in singing "Jesus Christ, Superstar," light all around. Externally, nothing happened but the fall of rain. Internally, Jesus held me. Deep inside, it was his whisper I heard, it was his love that told me, "I have been waiting so long for you." All an observer would have seen was a weeping man standing, looking up at the rain. All I saw was Him. All I felt was Him, providing hope in my hopelessness. Where guilt had been tyrant, His grace brought freedom. Where I saw no future, His future for me was good. Being held by Him is good. Walking with Him is good. It's good to be His.[4]

Well, back then I was Mike in that "filthy soul" stage, mired in the muck of my life. Like him, I had two choices: self-destruction or receiving Jesus' embrace. Conversion is when you turn

---

[4] Howerton, Mike. *Miles to Cross: A Spiritual Journey on the Open Road.* Relevant Books, 2004. 141

from one choice and choose another. Mike and I both chose Jesus' embrace.

For me, that embrace had begun even before the Coney Island experience which I am about to describe. There was my grandfather's prayer, which had seemed to bring Jesus right into the room. My church's open-armed welcome of me at my worst mirrored the unconditional love given to the Prodigal Son in Jesus' parable. But the deciding moment came during my summer job that year. I worked for the old New York Bible Society, organizing door-to-door distribution of free scriptures in every conceivable language. Believe me, this was not a merit-based job; I was not hired for my holiness.

I crisscrossed New York City from Flatbush to Morrisania to Bushwick to the boardwalk on Coney Island. In those days Coney Island was a major amusement park next to the beach, and I was nestled in between the sausage and peppers stand and the bathhouse. Each day I stood on the boardwalk and gave away free portions of the Bible, usually the Psalms and the Gospel of John, as people came off the subway heading toward the beach. Don't picture anything like the Jehovah's Witnesses or Mormon missionaries at your front door; I did not have a nice spiel or presentation, I just handed stuff out.

Jesus' embrace came quickly. It was while distributing those Bibles that I came face-to-face with the power that lay within those pages. Reactions were strong. Some people took the Bible, spit at me, hit me. Some took the Bible to the beach and came back hours later to hug me, kiss me, and thrust money into my hand. Like Paul on the Damascus Road I was being slapped around by reality, and the reality was that this Bible must really be something. Just because of that book, I found perfect strangers hating me, and others loving me. Embracing me. Like Paul, I was startled and left to think about it.

That night, lying in bed, I said, "Dear God, if you exist, and I don't think you do . . ." I have no idea how the prayer went on, but it was a first step, and eerily similar to Mike Howerton's anguished challenge to God.

Years later, this poem emerged from that halting prayer.

Conversion
(John 21:15-17)

"Dear God,
if you exist,
and I don't think you do..."

   that was my midnight prayer
   peeling away the layers
   of my indifference
   the dark night of my soul
   uttered as a silent scream
   angry, frustrated, and mean,
   but never finished
   because, with that, it began.
   Would I shake my fist at Nothing?
   Or shout at No One?
   Can't fervor be the fire of faith?!
   From that uncertain spark of anger
   grew a certain sense of danger
   a willing riskiness
   to leap beyond the boundaries of unworthiness.
   Not quite blinded by the Damascus road light,
   not quite fed by Emmaus' bread,
   not, like Thomas, revived by Jesus' bleeding side
   but lost enough to be found
   more like Peter, by love unbound.[5]

---

[5] Rowe, David Johnson. *Fieldstones of Faith, Vol. I.* Lulu Press, 2005. 17

If St. Paul's conversion has been forever known as the "Damascus Road conversion," mine can be the "Coney Island Boardwalk conversion." Both imply that there is one transformative moment in which you are converted from one kind of person into another. While I am sure that there truly are sudden conversions, just as there surely are people who fall in love at first sight, my guess is that, more often than not, even for St. Paul, conversion is a process. Things happen along the way that we may not put together right away. Then we do, and we are believers. The difference between believers and non-believers is often just the willingness to connect the dots. For believers, things happen and you begin to see a pattern, a theme, a nudge, a direction; you start to think it is God trying to get your attention. For non-believers the same things happen but are dismissed as coincidence, luck, random.

For me, back then, the dots were getting clearer and bolder, from being kicked out of college straight to Coney Island. Something was happening. I was being moved to make a change.

I liken it to Moses' encounter with the famous "burning bush" (Exodus 3:2-4). While in the wilderness Moses sees a bush that seems to be on fire but it is not being consumed. Intrigued, he walks over and finds God. God tells Moses to go to Egypt, and tell Pharaoh, "let my people go." The rest is history, but it began with Moses connecting the dots. He noticed the bush, took the bait, met God, and saved his people. I have often wondered how many other people had walked right by that same burning bush. Maybe they didn't take notice. Or care. Or couldn't be bothered. Or explained it away. Whatever the case, they missed their chance for a one on one with God, with destiny, with the immortality that Moses enjoys because he bothered to connect the dots.

After my Damascus Road encounter on the Coney Island Boardwalk I was determined not to miss the burning bush

God seemed to be putting in my path. I connected the dots, I was ready to change. Conversion: check. Now what?

That was when I started on the path to Church. If God was that tireless in chasing me, it was time to stop running away, and instead change direction. And for me the direction to head was toward Church. Go to seminary, become a pastor, and do what I had seen my father and grandfather do: it seemed obvious. My "call" was that simple.

Church embodied the embrace of Jesus. Or the embrace of Jesus was the Church. The Church was my grandfather with his hand on my head, and the people of Pilgrim Congregational Church who welcomed me home, and the strangers on the boardwalk who hugged me, and the Bible that hit people so hard, and the God who was inherent in my atheist prayer and didn't take offense.

So I turned not only toward God but also toward Church, the Church family and Church Universal that had been there all along. There's a saying, "If you look around for God and can't find God, guess who moved!" It's a statement, not a question. It was I who had moved, who had been away, distant, apathetic, dismissive of God and Church. They had been faithful, always there, ready. Embraceable.

In college I sometimes rolled out of bed and stumbled into The First Baptist Church of Hamilton, New York. Hamilton was a small town, Colgate a small college. My exploits and indiscretions were surely known and probably observed by half the people in that church. Yet this scraggly, longhaired, hung over 1960s hippie was always warmly welcomed. People greeted me, shared their hymnbooks, led me by the hand to coffee hour. No one ever seemed repulsed, perplexed, put off or judgmental. I was there, they were there, God was there. That is Church.

Years later Colgate invited me to come back and speak at three events organized by the university chaplains. Alida called it the "David Rowe Redemption Tour." We stopped at every scene of my thousand and one sins. Our last stop was at The First Baptist Church. I needed to say thank you to a church that had known how to be Church at a time when a troubled young man really needed Church even if he didn't know it.

That is the kind of church I was turning toward. Much later in my life, when it seemed I had again hit bottom, I again turned toward a church of my youth. It was in 1991, when, on the day after Easter, I was fired from my dream job. In my overheated imagination that Easter Monday, it seemed to me that my crucifixion came after the Resurrection! Being fired can make you that self-absorbed.

Until that day in 1991 I had had a near perfect pastoral career. I had served churches in Massachusetts and New York, we experienced growth and success every step of the way. Along the way I got deeply involved in world mission, which led me to Millard Fuller's Habitat for Humanity, then in its infancy. While still a pastor I became President of Habitat during its years of phenomenal growth worldwide and finally made the leap to working for Habitat fulltime, a dream come true. I was Millard's right hand man. Unfortunately, his multiple sexual harassments caught up to him, he did not appreciate being confronted, and all of us who stood up for the women were fired.[6]

My perfect career came to an abrupt halt. I was living in a remote, rural southwestern Georgia town, looking for a job, finding myself blackballed. Rejections piled up. Fighting discouragement and anger, I would head north every few months

---

[6] Rowe, David Johnson. *My Habitat for Humanity.* Lulu Press, 2011

scrounging for interviews. On one job-hunting trip, at a particularly low point on my odyssey, I decided to go back to my old childhood neighborhood in Queens. I went there for inspiration, looking for a reminder of when things seemed simpler, purer, things like life and God and faith and Church.

I parked my car in front of our old house, and started walking. My father's Pilgrim Congregational Church was right on the corner, still white stucco with black trim, a place of a million memories, and those memories accompanied me on my walk. I visited the parks and playgrounds, the ball field and P.S. 90, the pizza place and the deli, the apartment houses and backyards and front stoops of friends, the overhead subway we called "The El," the old movie theater and ice cream parlor, the pool hall.

Surprisingly, every step and every memory turned me back to that little church. We didn't think of it as a little church. For us in the 50s and 60s it was the center of the universe, Jerusalem and the Vatican and Mecca all wrapped up in stucco on the corner of 104th Street and 89th Avenue. Everything important happened there, or at least everything that happened there was important.

Suddenly I was at peace. I knew what I wanted. I was still fired, still blackballed, but no longer desperate. I had a focus, a purpose, and a destination. I knew in that instant that all I needed was to get a church, any church, and get back to doing Church. It didn't matter the size or the salary or the location. I had been too obsessed with restoring my name, reputation, and career trajectory, as a sort of revenge. Don't they say that the best revenge is looking good? I had been determined to end up looking good professionally. But going back to Queens cleared my head. I knew what I needed. I knew what I wanted. Church.

With a cleared head and a new focus maybe I interviewed better. I stopped being a raging, frantic, vengeful candidate. Instead, I was someone who only wanted to carry on the family business in as simple and humble a way as my father and grandfather had done.

The First Baptist Church of Pittsfield, Massachusetts pulled me out of the dumpster, dusted me off, took a gamble, and set me free to work. Then Greenfield Hill Congregational Church came into my life, bringing me full circle to the Congregationalism of my youth. Two churches that knew how to do Church right. Two churches with a deep commitment to youth, a desire to make a difference through mission, old-fashioned priorities like Sunday School and pastoral care, demanding and expectant with preaching, no frills, no rigmarole, no pettiness.

Just Church. The family business.

THREE

What is Church?

Church!
We're gonna have church today
turn frowns around
send worries away
take fear to task
the worst can't last
we're gonna have Church today.

That little poem has been bouncing around my head for many years, inspired by a Sunday morning visit to an African American church in Americus, Georgia. At the time, I was Director of Operations at the headquarters of Habitat for Humanity, International, and this church was one that several of our staff members attended. One day their pastor died suddenly. He was young, energetic, beloved, and now gone. My intention was to attend an hour or two of church, pay my respects, and show my support.

I came prepared with some thoughts to help a congregation of grief-stricken, heartbroken, sorrowful people. My hope was to bring what the Bible calls "the peace which passeth all understanding" (Philippians 4:7), some words of comfort and commiseration. That was my plan.

Instead, I entered a church full of joy and celebration! The pastor's chair and the pulpit were covered with white ribbons and white banners. The pastor's wife was regally dressed in white from head to toe. There was not a mournful tone, not a single mourner's black dress. I quickly changed my message.

Church owned the day, not death. I titled an earlier book *Death Is Defeated*, echoing the promise of St. Paul, that "the last enemy to be defeated (destroyed) is death" (1 Corinthians 15:26). My book was reaching for that promise. That Americus church was living the promise.

What is Church? Church at its best is what I saw that day in Georgia, a place where people gather together to live the promises of faith. I look at Church from two viewpoints: Church at its best and at its most basic. At its most basic Church is a gathering. The concept of church comes from the Greek word *ekklesia*, which historically was simply a town meeting. Jump ahead from ancient Greece to today and my Greenfield Hill Congregational Church is located on Meeting House Lane. In towns across New England a church was known as the Meeting House. In some rural towns the annual town meeting is still held at the local church that sits by the town square. Church is a gathering.

Church is one of those words, or concepts, with several layers of meaning. It can be a building. Or an experience. An institution. A focus of ritual, a treasure trove of tradition, a keeper of doctrine.

Church can be my little gem of New England architecture up on a hill in somewhat rural Connecticut, or the billion plus people gathered under the banner of Roman Catholicism.

Church can be a sacred place, a fellowship, a community, a school for learning and teaching and for all the really big questions.

Church can be a family, an enterprise, a brand, a denomination, a destination, a starting point.

Church manages somehow to be a noun but seem like a verb. It is the strange and wonderful amalgamation of being and doing. When Church is done right it can be hard to distinguish the noun from the verb.

After having Church one Sunday morning here at Greenfield Hill, I headed across the lawn to our coffee hour just as

Sunday School let out. A little girl came running up to me, full of joy and energy and excitement. "I had soooo much fun inside that building," she declared, pointing to our Sunday School building. Like a journalist stumbling upon a good story, I decided to grill her with the *who, what, where, when, and why* of Journalism 101. I wanted to know what went on in that building for fifty minutes that could bring such delight.

"I like it!" she explained, as if explanation wasn't necessary. "I like the teachers, I like the people, I like God."

She had just experienced Church, noun and verb. Church as place, Church as experience, Church as being, Church as doing, Church as people. And she liked it.

What's not to like? Unfortunately, plenty. Two thousand years have given Church ample opportunity to fail miserably, usually fueled by arrogance.

I once saw a tiny church in upstate New York, which proclaimed itself on its signboard, "The Only True Christian Church." Years later when I was pastoring a Baptist Church, a new family started attending and wanted to join. As was the custom I contacted their home church in Mississippi, also Baptist, and asked for a Letter of Transfer. The Mississippi pastor responded that they did not issue transfer letters to "churches outside their faith"! In the same vein for centuries the Roman Catholic Church proclaimed "no salvation outside the Church," referring only to itself as "The Church."

Thankfully, much of that has changed. But as recently as my growing up days and into my early years in ministry Catholics and Protestants were still excluding one another from heaven, and the hurt of division lingers. Such single-minded arrogance can be annoying and insulting on one level. On another level it has been inflammatory and cruel, leading to inquisitions, wars, slavery, abuse, intolerance, and holocaust.

Yet I love Church.

In one of the more fanciful descriptions of Church St. Peter calls us "a Royal Priesthood, a Holy Nation, a Peculiar People" (1 Peter 2:9, KJV). Royal, holy, and peculiar. He was right, we are an odd mix, but when it works it works well.

After writing my book *Faith at Work* I was invited to do a lot of workshops on the topic of work and faith. In the workshops I used a wonderful poem that I can neither locate nor remember fully. The best I can do is an approximation.

> *Work!*
> *The love of it.*
> *The sound of it,*
> *the smell*
> *the sweat*
> *the effect of it*
> *the feel*
> *the pulse*
> *the beat of it*
> *the need*
> *the work*
> *the pay of it.*
> *Work!*

That is Church for me. In a humble echo of that mostly lost poem I can say:

> *Church!*
> *I love it.*
> *The work, the people, the place of it,*
> *the pews, the altar, the pulpit of it,*
> *the ideas, the feel, the concept of it,*
> *the praying, preaching, teaching,*
> *the ritual, the routine,*
> *the smells and bells,*

the history and tradition of it,
the heroics and humility of it.
Church!
I love it.

St. Peter was right. Church is royal, holy, and peculiar. Church comes in all sizes, shapes, and styles as people have sought an effective connection with God. In Paris I experienced two churches, almost side by side, that captured the grandeur and the folly of Church.

On our honeymoon, Alida and I went to two cities: she took me to Paris, where she had been before, and I took her to my beloved Prague. The trip was an extravaganza of art, architecture, history, beauty, and Church. We began our first day in Paris walking across the River Seine to visit the 13th-century Sainte-Chapelle and the 12th-century cathedral, Notre Dame.

Notre Dame was magnificent, impressive, and formidable. It was also worshipful, spiritual, uplifting. Notre Dame seems almost to be smiling, confident, sure of itself and its place in the world. It hearkens back to a time when cathedrals dominated the landscape in Europe just as church steeples dominate the landscape in New England. There was a collective assurance, a creed in architecture that pronounced to the world, "Here we are. This is important! You want to know God? You want to feel close to God? Come in."

Despite the majesty of Notre Dame it did not feel arrogant, just self-evident, offering itself as the embodiment of the universal truth of the Gospel. I admit that I went in as a tourist, but I came out as a worshipper. Notre Dame was alive with faith even with the throngs of tourists circling the sanctuary nave, listening to their audio tours. I have now visited Notre Dame countless times and it is always the same. The side chapels attracted worshippers who stopped for prayer, lit candles, gazed reverently at sacred art and sculpture. People lined up for confession. The main sanctuary was alive with worshippers participating actively in the Mass. It was Church, open for business.

We left Notre Dame and headed to the Sainte-Chapelle. Holy Chapel. A stained glass extravaganza telling countless Bible stories. In addition, there are sculptured friezes of more Bible stories on an outside balcony. The whole experience is one of breathtaking beauty, extraordinary art, and Biblical interpretation. Altogether, it should be one amazingly inspiring experience.

Except.

Except this lovely little holy chapel was built for the personal use of King So-and-so and Queen What's-her-name. What's more, it was built to house a piece of Jesus' cross and his crown of thorns. In other words, it was the private reliquary of two of the most important relics in the whole Christian world, stuck in a private chapel just for Mr. and Mrs. King and Queen. And maybe their kids. Nobody else. Because downstairs, under the Sainte-Chapelle, is another little chapel for the rest of the palace staff. Unlike the welcoming majesty and joy of Notre Dame, the Sainte-Chapelle seemed to say, "go away, this is private, you don't count."

I could almost imagine old King Louis, the original Saint Louis, proud of the fact that his Sainte-Chapelle was now a tourist trap charging admission. Look, don't touch. Don't make a connection. Keep the line moving.

I admit, this is overly-critical, my personal reaction. There is no denying the beauty of Saint Louis' Chappelle, nor the likelihood that many visitors are deeply and spiritually blessed by faith on such beautiful display. But I was struck by the contrast between what Christianity once was, or had a chance to be, and what is has become. The Notre Dames of the world were built to be places of power and influence, spiritual and temporal. They made a statement of strength, importance, universality, eternity, even ultimate triumph. Everything else pales by comparison.

Meanwhile the Sainte-Chapelles of the world mimic the vanity and selfishness and insensitivity of too much that passes for religion. Comparing these two magnificent structures, Notre Dame and the Sainte-Chapelle, reveals the disconnect between what Christ's Church claims to be and what we too often turn out to be. We claim to be God's house. We settle for being a private chapel, or a tourist trap.

Not every church is Paris' Notre Dame in architecture but we are Notre Dame in purpose. Our God is the same, our Gospel of Good News is the same, our claim to Jesus Christ is the same.

Thirty years ago I started a mission called Friends of Christ in India (FOCI), partnering with my Indian friend, Azariah. Among our many works we helped to build about twenty churches. I named the first one "Emmanuel" in honor of the first church I pastored, up in Mechanicville, New York. The other I named "Redeemer," suggested by my grandfather, Linwood Rowe. But after I had gotten that hubris or vanity out of my system, Azariah insisted that all the other churches be called "Christ Church." Plain. Simple. Clear. Period. In effect, we are all Christ Church, or we are no church at all. We are not the King's private chapel, no matter how precious his relics might be.

I am not an expert on Parisian anything, much less church life. I am merely taking a stab at grasping how an institution that began as the Bride of Christ could eventually become an anachronism in many parts of the world. Outdated. Underutilized. Dwindling. Empty. Turned into restaurants, museums, private homes, concert halls.

Something went sour. Enough so that when various French revolutions took place Church clergy were slaughtered and churches closed. Somehow the churches had ended up on the side of Kings with their private stained glass chapels holding the Crown of Thorns rather than with the people whose lives felt like a crown of thorns was pressed down on their heads.

Thankfully, some people, enough people, are able to see the genuine truth within the Church despite the excesses of those who abuse the Church. Sort of like being able to actually enjoy the rose despite all the prickly thorns.

I fear that I may have overdrawn this comparative analogy of Notre Dame and the Sainte-Chapelle. Europe already suffers the reputation of being "post-Christian," filled with breathtaking but empty churches. That is not entirely true. On another visit to Paris we attended two Catholic churches, one in the morning and one in the evening. Both sanctuaries were full, the spirit of worship was vibrant.

In Prague I found vibrant worship and faithful worshippers in several churches. In Belgrade I went to midweek early morning worship at four Serbian Orthodox churches, and there was a steady stream of people coming to worship. Venice and Budapest offered similar proof of people practicing their faith in Church. These may not be the good old days, but there is life in those old bones, yet. Church is somehow greater than our human folly and failure.

My experiences of Church in Prague led to this poem:

The Gates of Hell
(Matthew 16:18)

Across peaceful and hostile lands
spires still inspire
The Church still stands
atheists do their best

to lambaste
religion's excess
nevertheless
The Church
with capital "C"
us, we
still stand
and withstand
every
adversary.

The Nazis and Communists
have come and gone
no need to be afraid
I saw their May Day Parade

Once, yes,
they did suppress
and in time may try again
to mock or oppress
yet
the Church still stands
Gothic, Baroque, whatever
it does matter
the Church is structure
>>> *girth*
>>> *heft*
>>> *power*
Presumed, assumed, exhumed,
Power, symbol and time
beyond fear
when yesterdays are past
the Church is still here.

The Gates of hell
cannot prevail.[7]

Maureen Dowd, an Op-Ed columnist for the New York Times, was working on a column despairing about the Catholic Church. She called former New York Governor Mario Cuomo to get his take. He told her, "if the church were my religion, I would have given it up a long time ago. All the mad and crazy popes we've had... all the terrible things the church has done. (But) Christ is my religion, the church is not."[8] Cuomo was talking about his own Roman Catholic Church but he could just as well have been referring to any and every stripe of Christianity, each with our own scandals and abuses and excesses. The Bible could have been referring to the history of all religion when it said, "All have sinned and fall short of the glory of God" (Romans 3:23). Humility helps.

When I was studying for my Doctorate one of the required courses was on "Church." The professor remarked, "The proof that the Church really is the Bride of Christ is that after two thousand years of really lousy leadership the Church still stands." In other words, there is something in the experience of Church that is both above and beyond the mere attempts of humans to make something of it.

When people talk about Church they often end up discussing the merits of "High Church" versus "Low Church." High Church means formal, ritualized, often directed by a prayer book or missal, with a set liturgy and proscribed prayers. Everything in good order, nothing left to chance, not much room for spontaneity. Low Church, then, is informal,

---

[7] Rowe, David Johnson. *Fieldstones of Faith, Vol. II.* Lulu Press 2008

[8] *New York Times,* May 20, 2012, A11.

spontaneous. It can be creative, even a bit edgy. There are few rules, few boundaries. But that is surface stuff: whether a church service style is too long or too short, too loud or too quiet, too rigid or too free form. The real issue is what Church does seven days a week, not how it sounds on Sunday. Substance, not style.

I insist on calling myself "High Church" as a way of emphasizing high standards, great expectations, profound demands. To have a high view of Church is to have a lofty view, to expect the best, to want the best, to be the best. To be the best requires three perspectives. First, what does God call us to be? Second, what do people need us to be? Third, what can we be to the best of our ability?

Number three allows us to be realistic. When the Church acts to the best of our ability, even to the best of our collective ability, there is still stuff we can't do. We can't raise the dead. We can't solve the Middle East or Israel/Palestine crisis. We can't end war. Yet.

Despite St. Paul's wonderful promise, "I can do all things through Christ who strengthens me" (Philippians 4:13), and Jesus' daring promise that his followers will be able to do "greater things" (John 14:12), there are limits on Church.

But not as many as we think, not as many as we settle for, not as many as we assume. Functioning to the best of our ability, the Church can look at what God calls us to be and people need us to be and achieve some surprising things. Some are literal, some are figurative.

In the literal category are food and shelter. Jesus' mandate to feed the hungry is absolutely clear. Or is it? Amazingly, I have encountered some who insisted otherwise.

In 1975 I was about to take my first mission trip overseas, to Africa. It was still a big deal in those days, and a neighboring pastor came by to wish me well. He wanted to know what I would be doing and was quite pleased when I mentioned visiting missionaries, encouraging African pastors, preaching in churches. He shook my hand vigorously to affirm my mission. However, when I mentioned that the impetus was the horrific famine in Africa and apartheid in South Africa, the pastor literally dropped my hand like it was too hot to handle. He then lectured me on the real meaning of Jesus' call to "feed the hungry ... feed my sheep." "Feed them spiritually, that's what Jesus meant," he told me quite forcefully. "Preach, teach, tell the Good News of Salvation, give out evangelistic tracts, distribute Bibles. That's what Jesus meant."

So much for the "literal" interpretation of the Bible he espoused. When I suggested that Jesus actually said "feed" over and over again to Peter, and that Jesus may well have at least partially meant actually feeding real people, the good church pastor left. No exaggeration. He turned around, walked out.

Blessedly, churches have still worked hard to feed the hungry, locally and globally. From food pantries to "soup kitchen" community meals, a church like ours makes sure that the poor and the hungry have a chance to eat a good meal. That's in the literal category of fulfilling a Biblical mandate in a way that meets God's expectations, people's needs, and our ability.

Shelter is another area. In the book about my years with Habitat for Humanity, *My Habitat for Humanity: The Mostly Good Old Days*[9], I described Jesus' specific demands in Matthew 25 to feed the hungry, clothe the naked, visit the lonely, give water to the thirsty, as Jesus' "for instance list." Jesus was outlining a life of mission for his Church saying, "for instance, feed the hungry, visit the lonely." It wasn't meant as the final word but as a good place to start.

---

[9] Rowe, David Johnson. *My Habitat for Humanity.* Lulu Press, 2011

His deeper teaching was to look at "the least of these" among us and around us, and to do whatever was possible to lessen their least-ness. What Habitat rightly did was to expand Jesus' "for instance list" to include housing. Ergo, "feed the hungry, clothe the naked, find shelter for the needy." Affordable housing. Available housing. Transitional housing. Decent apartments. Safe shelters.

For some Christians that may mean lobbying and advocating, set asides and tax incentives, mortgage and foreclosure help.

For Habitat-oriented churches it has meant using a free Saturday, a college spring break, a summer vacation, or retirement days to work at a local Habitat project, pounding nails, cutting wood, mixing cement. The end result is a literal fulfillment of scripture.

For the figurative interpretation of scripture, I give credit to evangelical mega-church pastor Tim Keller and his book *Generous Justice*[10]. He tackles some of Jesus' more startling successes like giving sight to the blind, raising the dead, and telling the paralytic to get up and walk. Keller dares us to expand our definition of what it means to enable folks to see, or to set free the prisoner, or even to resurrect the dead. People are blind to all sorts of things, Keller reminds us. We can be dead in many ways, spiritually dead, emotionally dead, dead to hope and faith and love. We can be paralyzed in lots of ways, by fear or indecision. We can be imprisoned by addictions and obsessions, walled in without walls, held captive without guards.

With such broadened definitions the Church can now dare to follow the path set by Jesus, a path that definitely leads us

---

[10] Keller, Timothy, *Generous Justice: How God's Grace Makes Us Just.* Riverhead Books, 2010.

to the blind, the imprisoned, the paralyzed, the dead. "High Church" for me means that we really take that path.

In my pastoral career one of my toughest ministries has been with people with addictions, whether it is alcohol or drugs, behavior or habits, food or tobacco. Using those broadened definitions it is safe to say that some addicts have the full range of Jesus' suggested needs for ministry- they can seem blind, paralyzed, imprisoned, and dead. Imprisoned by their addiction, blind to what it is doing to others as well as to themselves, paralyzed by the fear of losing old and familiar ways of facing life, dead to feelings and entreaties, theirs is a personal destruction on a grand scale. Everything is hurting. Everything needs healing. Trust is gone, respect is lost, promises are not believed. Life is a dead end.

Can Church change that, literally or figuratively? Can Church raise the dead, set the prisoner free, help the blind to see? On any level? By any definition?

My Grandfather Linwood had the touch with alcoholics. With his combination of good ol' country boy instincts, his imminent return of Jesus theology and his personal journey of redemption, he could help folks with their blindness, their paralysis, their shackles, even their deadness.

That is a God-given gift, and I don't have it. But the beautiful power of Church is that it is a gathering place for all sorts of God-given gifts. What I've done is to take my grandfather's faith, my father's wisdom, and my own experience to enable Church to be a place of deliverance. More importantly, I have used the wonderful array of gifts within my church family to touch people who need deliverance. Their wisdom and experience often fuels a faith that is more effective in delivering the hope and healing so urgently needed. Through the intervention, example and guidance of Church members, many have been restored to living a full life.

"Deliverance" is a deliberate choice of words. In most cities you can find churches with the word "deliverance" in their name, Deliverance Tabernacle, Deliverance Church of God. They promise to help you to take on the very enemies that threaten to imprison you, blind or paralyze you, even kill you spiritually and physically. By prayer, anointing, laying on of hands, even by exorcism they will "deliver" you from what threatens you and, "plant your feet on higher ground."

We may not all use the language of demons and possession and exorcism. But when people are suffering and in urgent need they can feel like they are under attack from forces beyond their control. The purpose of Church is to be so forcefully present that no one feels alone.

Together, Church wrestles boldly with all the demons that bedevil us. The catalogue of demons we face can seem endless, but so is the catalogue of gifts we have at our disposal. We come up against addiction, poverty, sickness, despair, injustice, sorrow, brokenness, loss, failure, and plain old meanness. But we go after them with all the tools of faith. St. Paul describes our tools in the language of battle, reminding the Church that we have "the full armor of God so that you can take your stand against the devil's schemes... with the belt of truth, the breastplate of righteousness, the gospel of peace, the shield of faith, the helmet of salvation, the sword of the spirit." And then Paul adds, "plus prayer" (Ephesians 6:11, 14-18). That is impressive, empowering, downright invigorating.

Being Church can seem isolated and overwhelming, as if we are outgunned, outmanned, outmaneuvered. We are not. Whether it was my grandfather going up against the "devil's schemes" of addiction, or Martin Luther King Jr. up against the "devil's schemes" of racism, or Mother Teresa up against the "devil's schemes" of horrific poverty, Church proved surprisingly forceful.

It took me a long time to fully grasp the true power of Church. Too often I could be shy, apologetic, hesitant about inserting Church into the lives and problems of people, only to discover that Church was what they wanted and needed. Unfortunately, we are all limited by too narrow a definition of Church. A popular folk hymn dares us to broaden our definition:

> The Church is not a building,
> the Church is not a steeple,
> the Church is not a resting place,
> the Church is the people.

Then, in a joyous, optimistic refrain the hymn boldly declares,

> I am the Church.
> You are the Church.
> We are the Church together.
> All across the nation,
> all around the world,
> Yes we're the Church together.[11]

That is High Church thinking. Great expectations, great demands, great standards. When Church fails, or falls, that is us failing or falling. When Church is dynamic, real, a place of honest to goodness deliverance, that is also us. We are The Church Together, yes, with capitals.

I learned the power of Church slowly but steadily. When I finally got converted and decided to go to seminary my father took me under his professional wing. He was a pastor in Flatbush, Brooklyn, and arranged for five churches to hire me to do Summer Ministry. It was the summer of 1968 and everyone was panic driven to connect with kids. We did bus trips to

---

[11] Avery, Richard and Marsh, Donald. *We Are the Church.* Hope Publishing Co., 1972.

Mets games, Vacation Bible School, endless basketball, anything and everything to get kids off the streets.

That led to opening The Growing Concern Coffee House in the church basement. To enter the teenagers had to turn over drugs and guns to me for safekeeping. The evenings included folk music, hipster poetry, antiwar films, all sorts of protest and activism. Mostly, it was "anything goes," including bad language and ribald humor.

Me? I sort of hung back, I certainly didn't force myself or my faith on anyone. To my utter amazement that really bothered the kids. Here was the one safe place in Brooklyn where anyone could "do their own thing" and the only person not doing their own thing was me.

It was put to me very bluntly. "Why don't you care about us?" asked one high school kid. "You open this place, you let everybody sing, speak, do whatever. But you never tell us what's important to you. I think you don't trust us."

That shook me. I was trying so hard to relate, to be open, to not offend, to make room for every thought, word, and deed. The only thing missing was me. And the kids noticed.

The next Friday I told my story. After the Doors' new album and before the Leonard Cohen movie I took the stage and told them my journey from gangs to booze to expulsion to the Coney Island Boardwalk all the way to conversion. Jesus. God. Church. Faith.

This opened a whole new world in ministry and their response was provocative to say the least. Some of them offered to let me keep their drugs. Later that night a young friend brought in an air conditioner he had just stolen because I had mentioned how hot it was in my parent's house. These well-intentioned gestures reminded me that yes, conversion is a process, and so is Church. It is not one thing, but a combination and accumulation of quite different things. We are never in it alone. For the record, we flushed the drugs and returned the air conditioner.

St. Paul definitely knew what he was talking about when he stated, "The body is a unit, though it is made up of many parts; and though all of its parts are many, they form one body. So it is with Christ" (1 Corinthians 12:12). The body Paul is referring to is Church, we are "the body of Christ" (1 Corinthians 12:27), one body, many parts, singular and plural at the same time.

He goes on in an almost humorous vein to imagine how a body functions if the various parts lose their focus or perspective, if they fall victim to pride or arrogance, if they stop doing their unique task and envy the gifts of others. "Yes, we're the Church together," or we are just laughable.

When I started Andover-Newton Theological School I did a series of youth pastor jobs near Boston. I taught Sunday School, led youth groups, started drop-in centers, found runaways, did drug and draft counseling, a veritable smorgasbord of ministry.

And I opened another Growing Concern Coffee House, in the basement of Newton Highlands Congregational Church. An immediate success, we caught the attention of the local mafia wannabees. One Friday night the gang came in, beat the heck out of me and my partner, and smashed the place up. I was about to find out, again, the power of Church.

The Church Deacons asked to meet with me the next day. Instead of shutting us down and sending me packing, the Church practically demanded that I reopen the coffee house, promising full support. One Deacon, a distinguished and successful businessman, said he would come to help.

The next Friday he rolled up on his motorcycle and walked into our coffee house with his leather jacket and big boots, ready to relate. No one would go near him. "That's not Mr. Jones," a few of the teenagers told me, "that's not really him."

Chagrined but determined, my Mr. Jones returned the next week, coming straight from work, dressed in his three-piece pinstripe suit, carrying his briefcase. The young people swarmed to be with him. Now he was the real Mr. Jones. Now he could relate.

St. Paul wrote that he was willing to be "all things to all people that by all means I might save some" (1 Corinthians 9:22), and no doubt that can include wearing leather. But it can also mean wearing the pinstripe suit and carrying your briefcase, if that is what is real, authentic. Sometimes the Church just needs to be Church to win some.

When I had both knees replaced I spent two weeks in the rehabilitation unit of a nursing home. I was there to be fixed, strengthened, rehabilitated, and motivated. For that to happen I needed different things at different times, even from different people. Sometimes it was ice, or meds, or physical therapy, or a Subway sandwich. Sometimes I needed to be pushed, given an example, or told to rest. There were even times when, in my own weakness, I needed to help others. In its own way, this was Church.

At my first physical therapy session the man in charge told me to stand up. I couldn't move. The guy next to me said, "Watch me," and he hoisted himself up on his walker. I looked at him: he had no legs. A few days later a new patient arrived, straight from the hospital, and refused to leave his room. I wanted to encourage him as others were encouraging me: I became a "wounded healer," as some people call Christians. I went to his room with my wounds and scars and weakness and even fear.

Guess what? It didn't work. But the next day he told the physical therapist he would try because, he said, "I don't want that preacher bugging me again!"

Church, like conversion, like any good therapy for the body or the soul, is a process. In the process we try anything. I love Notre-Dame and I love my quintessential New England Congregational Church. I love Sunday mornings and old Gospel hymns and weekly Bible Study. I love order and tradition and a decent dash of ritual.

But for the process to work we have to "move to where we are uncomfortable," as a great missionary told me. We can't be boxed in, rigid, predictable, out of touch, un-empathetic, un-imaginative, or just plain ornery.

That is why, despite my fairly ordinary, orthodox Church career, my ministry has taken me far and wide both within and outside the four walls of every Church I have served. From courtrooms to living rooms, from prison cells to accident scenes, from rehab centers to hospital beds, from front lawns to backyards we are Church. "Pop Up Markets" have become popular recently, much like the flash mob music videos where entire choruses and orchestras show up seemingly suddenly in surprising places, singing the "Hallelujah Chorus" or "Ode to Joy" in mall food courts and town squares. With Pop Up Markets, little temporary outposts of local stores "pop up" in parks, giving people a chance to taste their offerings.

Why not "Pop Up" Church or flash mob Church? Why not be Church seemingly suddenly in surprising places? Alida often remarks that if we really want to minister, we should not bother showing up at the Church office and instead spend our time at the supermarket and walking around downtown Fairfield. There is a reality to meeting people casually, unexpectedly, in the course of everyday activities that is different from meeting people in our office. Several times, encountering someone at a local restaurant, we have first learned of cancer diagnosis or cancer treatments, something that had not been told to us before or mentioned during our Sunday prayer concerns.

We regularly attend our young people's school activities, sitting in the stands with parents and siblings and friends. Conversation during a sixty minute lacrosse game is obviously more in-depth than the quick ten second handshake after Sunday service or a two minute catch up during coffee hour. Being at school concerts, Scout ceremonies, and during the "agony and ecstasy" of sports competitions allows us to be present in their lives on their turf doing what they like. Frankly, it deepens our relationships, and that carries over to when they are on our turf. Church is vitally important, but most of life is lived beyond the walls of a church building. So we need to get out.

After Pope Francis became Pope he began to stir things up not only among Catholics but also among all sorts of people who take faith and religion and God seriously. Like a wise old grandfather he gently chided religious folks for obsessing over certain hot potato socio-religious issues like homosexuality and abortion. Understanding that there are strong differences of opinion among genuinely earnest and spiritual folks, Pope Francis reminded us that Church is like a Field Hospital. A Field Hospital, whether near a battlefield or a disaster, takes all comers and takes them as they are.

That was Jesus' approach. If we proclaim that Church is "the body of Christ," in a way we are saying that Church is Christ, Christ is Church. For many people their first experience of Christ is going to be their experience of Church. We'd better be up to it.

The ultimate answer, then, to "What is Church," lies in the life of Jesus Christ. Church history, Church denominations,

Church battles and squabbles, Church saints and Church sinners are all instructive, good and bad. But the surest test of Church is measured by Jesus' life.

His was a life full of love, sacrifice, and faith. He said astounding things and did amazing things. He managed to exist within traditions and break boundaries. He paid attention to detail and never lost sight of the big picture. He was demanding and forgiving. His toughest rules he applied to himself. He did manage to fully embody the human and the divine. He lived in the present and pointed confidently to the future. He turned contradictions into paradoxes. He was religion and beyond religion. He was a living creed who needed no creed. Then he died, and didn't.

This is Church.

FOUR

Atheism, Art, and Inness

The Atheist and the Artist
(Psalm 14:1)

a fool's heart
is
devoid of God
  the artist's
  art
  fills the void
an atheist
knows
no creation by creator!
no design by designer?
that which is done
is not done
by anyone.
  the artist
  knows
  the divine spark
  blending here with there
  creates the art
  what's done is done
  by someone
for each
creation is a miraculous reach
something from nothing, or
nothing from something.

Being a pastor in the 21st century can feel a bit like owning an independent bookstore. You know books are important. You even know people who are still reading. But all around you the world of books has changed dramatically. Other independent bookstores have closed, even big chain bookstores have failed; the Kindle and e-books and the Internet have changed reading habits. Amazon rules the publishing world.

And so you sit in your quaint little bookstore, surrounded by words and ideas and authors that you value as friends, truly believing that you have just the right book for every person who passes by — if only they would come in. But more and more, the people pass by.

Paradoxically, every day provides more proof that what you believe in really is good, valuable, helpful, necessary. Old words and old ideas in old classics, and new words and new ideas in new stories, continue to inspire, challenge, provoke, teach. Everyone who comes into your bookstore somehow feels better, as though they were participating in something inherently good. Everyone who goes home with one of your books is glad they did.

Yet it is a struggle to stay open. Perhaps this is not a bad parable for Church in much of the world. We believe that what we have to offer is important; we still know people who share our belief. We actually do have a book that we are sure is right for every person passing by. We are confident that our old classic words and even our new stories have the power to transform and lift people to a good place.

Yet it remains a struggle to stay open. Certainly there are thriving churches and mega-churches. The landscape of America and Europe is still dotted with steeples and spires of churches and cathedrals. We still look good. But inside the paint may be chipping, the pews may be empty, the ministry may be shrinking.

Why? Atheism, some would immediately reply. I don't believe that. Atheism is only the latest excuse for the supposedly dwindling interest in Church. Through the years we have blamed the changing culture, changing demographics, changing lifestyle, changing priorities. Some would have us believe that there were "good old days" when Blue Laws kept Sundays sacred, prayer in public schools kept everyone pious, religions other than our own were out of sight and out of mind, and non-believers didn't speak up at all. Through such rose-colored glasses, Church life in 1650, 1750, 1850, 1950 was perfectly lovely. Everybody was church-going, Sunday-loving, and Sabbath-observing, so they say, until Madalyn Murray O'Hare came along and convinced the Supreme Court to kick prayer out of school.

Ever since, O'Hare's brand of aggressive, activist atheism has been blamed for the full range of social ills plaguing the universe. Once atheism won the Supreme Court, they won the classroom, they won teenagerhood and young adulthood, they won Hollywood and culture in general. With the defeat of prayer, and by extension God, western civilization headed straight downhill.

So the argument goes.

Consider two other possibilities. One, Christianity consistently shoots itself in the foot. Two, atheism is overblown. Or to put it another way, in Church most of our problems are of our own making, and as a defense mechanism we inflate the impact of atheism.

The failures of religion in general and the Church in particular are legion. We ran countries and empires for centuries, too often giving rise to oppression, excess, tyranny, intolerance. We had our chance and we blew it.

The British Empire was ruled by a King or Queen who literally headed the Church of England. The Holy Roman (Catholic) Empire ruled most of Europe. The Protestant Reformation led to official state churches in many countries. The Middle East has been ruled by Islam, India lurched from Hinduism to Islam and is now reasserting its Hindu primacy. Much of Latin America is identified as Catholic. Sri Lanka and Myanmar see their identity inexorably linked to Buddhism. Israel continues to wrestle with what it means to be a Jewish state. ISIS and Al Qaeda have made clear their singular vision of Islam as the only ruling principle in whatever land or state they establish. Orthodox Christianity and nationalism go hand-in-hand in Russia and the Balkans.

All over the world religion has had ample opportunity to prove itself as a force for good, a guiding principle, a natural leader, a moral exemplar. We have had opportunity, time, resources and power.

The fact that age by age and religion by religion we find people turning away, converting to something else, or choosing atheism ought to be the wake-up call. Ought to force us to look in the mirror. Ought to humble us. Ought to. Instead, we concentrate on scapegoats, whether atheism, secularism, liberalism or any ism other than ours.

For several years I audited courses at Harvard through their Divinity School and the Center for World Religions. One semester we took a field trip to a Hare Krishna Temple in Boston, held in a beautiful old townhouse on Commonwealth Ave. It was fascinating, colorful, joyous, exotic. And sad.

The twenty or so worshippers attended their god, Krishna, with pageantry and affection. Dancing, jumping, chanting, swaying, they gathered around the statue of Krishna. With modesty and devotion they undressed him, bathed him in a waterfall of ghee, purified butter, and ceremoniously dressed him again in what appeared to be fine silk.

Our professor, Dr. Diana Eck, was and is at the forefront of interfaith study and practice. She urges people to move beyond mere tolerance and, instead, to be willing to see the sacred in the worship of others, however different from our own. I was able to do that with the Hare Krishnas, to a degree. Issues of cultism and monotheism aside, these young people were clearly genuine in their devotion, they were experiencing the presence of their god in the idol, they were worshipful.

So, why was it sad? I couldn't take my eyes off the worshippers. With only slight exaggeration, they all appeared to be blonde, blue-eyed 20-somethings, fresh out of Kansas. When I talked to them later they sounded like they came from good ol' American church-going stock. I'm sure they grew up going to Sunday School and youth group, sang hymns by heart, got baptized and confirmed, acted in the Christmas pageant. In short, we had them, they were ours. Then we lost them.

Now they were jumping up and down in saffron robes, playing finger cymbals and dousing a Hindu idol with purified butter before playing dress up. It was hard not to feel that we had failed.

When I pastored The First Baptist Church of Pittsfield, I often brought Sunday worship to the county jail. The chapel was always packed, we were the only entertainment for the day. So, I was in a room packed with criminals, law breakers, they had all done something wrong, bad, hurtful. Trying to gauge their grasp of Bible knowledge and Christian ideals, early on I asked for a show of hands: how many grew up in Church? How many had been baptized? Gone to Sunday school? At every question every hand went up. Once upon a time we had them, they were ours. But we failed.

I read the obituary of a man whose father had been a Methodist pastor, and he considered becoming one. But, the obituary stated, he decided to devote his life to debunking the Bible and living a life without a god. Once again, we had him, he was one of us. But we lost him.

Yes, I do take this personally. Atheism is a denial of all that is at the center of my being. Atheism says that all that I believe in – all that I trust, do, hope for, all my inspiration and motivation and destination and occupation, all that I need and all that I yearn for – is not so. That is personal. And I don't blame atheism.

If someone has reached a decision for atheism on their own, I can respect that. But when they have been pushed to that conclusion by my own failure, evil, ineffectiveness, behavior, dullness, silliness, then, yes, I feel the loss personally.

The Christian Church has laid the foundation for most of the atheism I encounter. I have read a lot of the atheist books, listened to the debates, followed the growing movement, and talked with many who claim atheism. You don't have to dig too deep to see that the bulk of the problem is some mean pastor, some stuffy church, some harsh rule, some cruel event, some thoughtless dogma, some bad Christian, some prayer that wasn't answered, some God that seemed not to care.

Here is one story I am almost too ashamed to tell. In early June of 2015, during a "Q and A" on his own show, Pat Robertson was asked for advice on what to say to a woman whose three-year-old child had just died. His answer was an ugly spin on the old bromide "God knows best." Robertson's advice was to tell the grieving mother that her child could have grown up to be a Hitler or a Stalin, and beyond God's salvation. So God had done the child – and the mother – a *favor* by cutting short that life before it could turn to evil.

Let me be clear. Such horrific stupidity, bordering on blasphemy, may not always cause people to lose faith, or to quit on Church. But it surely causes people who are on the fence to look elsewhere.

To date, in my life, I have met only one true-blue, dyed-in-the-wool, full-throttled atheist. I do meet people who are angry with God, Church, clergy, religion, Christians. I am hardly the first to suggest that you can't be mad at something that doesn't exist. Passion against something is almost evidence that it is real to you. Atheism is the theological equivalent of what teenagers used to do when fed up with someone. They would put their hand up in the "stop" position and say to the person, "You are dead to me."

That seems like what is going on in much of atheism. The atheism that I experience is fed up with the Christianity of their experience, or the religion of their experience. They are saying to the Church, "You are dead to me."

That may actually be a greater threat to Church than total atheism. The late 1960s produced a "God is Dead" theology, complete with obituary. The 21st century version may be harsher, that God simply does not matter. Apathy. Irrelevance. I remember being told that in the world of physics inertia is more difficult to overcome than movement, even if in the opposite direction. If so, atheism is the movement in the opposite direction, and apathy is the inertia that is the tougher challenge.

Frankly, this is less of a problem for God than for Church. If God is, and if God is God, then God can handle our disinterest in a thousand creative ways. The Ten Plagues of Moses, Noah's flood, and manna from heaven are all good for short-term conversions. And there is always the angel of death. Christopher Hitchens notwithstanding, angry atheism often melts in the face of mortality. If God is, and if God is God, God ultimately wins.

There is no such guarantee for the Church. Our problem isn't atheism, but to coin a word: *aecclesiaism*. Life without Church. Now that's a movement. When the general population raises its collective hand in the "stop" position and says, "You're dead to me," that is our Armageddon.

Returning to the personal: when people try us and find us wanting, that is on us. That is not Madalyn Murray O'Hare's fault, or Hollywood's fault, or the fault of liberal college professors, as talking heads on television are fond of claiming.

In America and the West in general, the Church literally dominated the landscape, we owned the culture, we were the conversation, we had everyone's attention. That advantage was squandered. We lost it.

Any tourist wandering through Europe is met by a vast army of cathedrals, fortresses of faith. New England, my little corner of America, is famous for its steeples, with town squares presided over by churches, and usually a Church Street vying with Main Street for prominence. Even Brooklyn is nicknamed "the Borough of Churches." We are everywhere but, as a friend said, "our churches are a mile wide and an inch deep." Churches are emptying, dwindling, closing. And it isn't atheism's fault.

When I was younger pastors were always worried about "sheep stealing." Someone would leave another local church and join mine, and other clergy would call me a "sheep stealer." When someone left my church to attend somewhere else I accused them of "sheep stealing."

In reality, no one steals anybody's sheep. Sheep, a Biblical term for people, go where they are fed. If a church is feeding its people, the people stay. If not, they walk. In the old days they usually walked into another church. Nowadays, they might walk into apathy – just leave and not bother with Church anymore. Church is dead to them.

If Church is not worthwhile, people will fill their time with something else that is worth the while. Atheism is only the extreme end on the spectrum of finding something else. So, I'm not fighting atheism; I prefer to fight our own failures and the apathy that results. People want to believe.

From Atheism to … Art?

The bottom line is that people find God when and where they want to, and they don't find God when and where they don't want to. As I keep repeating, believers connect the dots, nonbelievers see no connection among the dots. Church exists to help folks connect the dots, to turn wonder into faith and practice. I can't argue anyone into faith. A good argument, something better than yelling at one another, is based on reason. However, much about faith is unreasonable. It is as unreasonable that Jesus walked on water as it is to accept his command to "forgive 70 times 7" (Matthew 18:21-22). Easter's resurrection is as unreasonable as to "turn the other cheek" (Matthew 5:39). Church oozes the unreasonable.

The best I can do is to tell what I know. Church life, especially old-fashioned Church life, makes good use of rituals called "witnessing" and "testifying," which mirror their use as legal terms. When we are called into court as a "witness," we are only permitted to "testify" to what we know firsthand. In the same vein, I am allowed to tell you my story, and in my story part of my faith comes from art. Art can be wonderfully convincing. Whether faith is inherent in the art, I can't say. I can say that art moves me with faith.

Believe me, I came late to art appreciation, having flunked it in college. Forty years later I stood before a Camille Pissarro painting at the Sterling and Francine Clark Museum in Williamstown, Massachusetts, stopped dead in my tracks, mesmerized. A year later, in the same museum, it was George Inness. Both led me by the hand on a wonderful journey of faith.

On one visit to the Clark for a special exhibit of new Inness acquisitions, I stood in the middle of the gallery, thankfully alone, so I could say out loud, "What are you saying to me?"

The Clark is a veritable cathedral of art, and the Inness gallery had all the feel of a chapel. It was a place for worship. So I invited God and Inness to talk with me. Inness would not have been surprised, nor God.

George Inness was an American landscape painter from the late 19th Century who turned pastoral scenes from New Jersey and New York into pastoral sermons. By design, that was his intention.

And yet, there is not a Biblical scene hinted at — no Biblical characters, not even Biblical themes. No Nativity, crucifixion, Abraham and Isaac, David and Goliath, Jesus teaching or healing. Nothing vaguely Biblical or overtly Christian.

Just trees, farmhouses, ponds, snow, autumn, sunsets, a wisp of smoke, a glimpse of people. In other words, God everywhere.

Inness was a Swedenborgian, a small Protestant Christian denomination with an emphasis on the mystical side of faith, a faith that permeates life. For Inness, his faith led him to want to paint in such a way that the viewer could sense, feel and know God better, clearer. For me, it works.

In the catalogue accompanying the Inness exhibit the curator states that, "Inness experimented with color, composition, and painterly technique in an attempt to present a vision of the natural world that transcends its physical appearance."[12]

In other words, there's more here than meets the eye, a basic argument for faith since time immemorial. There's more to paint than paint. There's more to trees than trees. There's more to creation than creation. There's more. Believe it.

I'm not arguing that art is the only way to God, or the best way. I am saying that if you are not afraid of faith, faith will find you in any of a million ways. Or more. The results can be inspiring, fun and surprising.

My addiction to Inness' art and the faith rush it gives me has led to obsession and humor. I catalogue my Inness sightings the way birders catalogue their birds.

During one Inness exhibit I kept returning to the gallery, finally grabbing one of those canvas chairs the museum provides and sitting myself at the perfect spot to view all the walls. Looking contemplative and scholarly, I thought, I took out my Pilot Pen and paper and began to write. "Stop!!" the gallery guard shouted, snatching away my pen. "What do you think you're doing? No pens are permitted in this museum."

I was mortified and ready to crawl away. But he persisted in wanting to know what I was up to. I muttered something about writing a book and having a chapter on the sacredness of Inness' art, adding in abject apologies.

"Well," he said to me, "that is good. But no pen." Turning to the crowd with authority, he announced, "This gentleman is a writer and he needs a pencil." Within moments I was amply supplied with pencils and my new friend, the guard, shooed people away from me. "He is a writer. He must have space." It was wonderfully embarrassing. The wonder made it worth the

---

[12] "George Inness: Gifts from Frank and Katherine Martucci," 2013

embarrassment. Wonder is definitely part of faith, and for many, that wonder comes through nature.

Whenever I ask people what convinces them that there is a God, the overwhelmingly number one answer is "nature." Many will go on to specify a sunset, the ocean, their backyard, a rainbow. The varieties and intricacies of nature are a powerful proof of God.

For most of my life I took nature for granted. One summer I led a Habitat for Humanity work camp to Puno, Peru. After an exciting train ride from Arequipa we arrived in Puno at night, and toured the worksite. I gathered the group for a peptalk, mini-sermon, instruction list, droning on until my son got my attention. "Dad, look up!" he said with the same kind of wonder I would find years later. "Look up."

I looked around at our group, and they were all looking up. Our worksite was on a high hill above Puno, which is 12,000 feet above sea level in the Andes. We were on one of the great rooftops of the world. When I finally looked up the stars that filled the heavens were so close it seemed we could touch them. For a few brief moments we stood there in awe. Then I reclaimed the spotlight and continued barking out orders for the next day's work. I actually said, as if to put the stars in their place, "Remember, we're here to work."

Well, actually, in the Habitat language of the day, we were there to show God's love, to be proof of God's presence. My son was simply pointing out that God's presence was already powerfully there. "Look up, Dad!"

It would be almost another twenty years before I started taking nature to heart, in nature and in art. It began with a chance encounter with Pissarro's painting, Saint-Charles Eragny (1891, Clark Museum). We had been in the museum a long time, my knees were killing me, I was probably grumpy, we were almost done. Walking down a long, narrow, unattractive gallery, there it was.

Moses had the Burning Bush, Elijah the still small voice, I had Pissarro daring me to look and think and feel deeper. My Pissarro obsession predated my Inness obsession, and I searched out his paintings and story with dogged determination.

To my amazement, he was an atheist. Maybe. He said he was, and that is his story, and he has as much right to his story as I do to mine. He was witness to his own unbelief, so I let it alone.

It was a young artist, the one mentioned in the poem at the start of this chapter, who dared me to see faith even in the atheism of Pissarro's art. "Maybe," the young artist said, "he couldn't keep God out of his art even if he wanted to. It's hard to be an artist and not believe."

That touched me. I thought back to my first visit to Prague. Greenfield Hill Church gave me a Sabbatical that I used for two purposes. I completed *Fieldstones of Faith,* a book of poetry based on scriptures, and I jumped into the world of religious art.

My goal with religious art was to look carefully at what the artist did with the particular Bible story being painted. I would stare at the facial expressions, look at the background, study the others in the scene. What was Caravaggio thinking or believing? Or Rembrandt, Michelangelo, the Masters known and unknown ("from the school of...," art labels often say), all the way to Chagall and Dali. In effect, I would let the Bible story speak to me afresh through the artist. And it always did.

In Prague, I stumbled across a whole museum of Chagall's Bible paintings, and another of Dali's many drawings based on Dante's Inferno. I couldn't believe what I was seeing, while at the same time, what I was seeing strengthened my believing.

Always I was asking, "What were you thinking, believing? What are you saying to me?" Even with Pissarro, even with his unbelief. Their art energized faith. Perhaps Pissarro could deny God with his words or writings, but he couldn't take God out of his gift, his craft, his art. Intended or not, I was feeling God in his art.

One Sunday in Prague I attended a Hussite Church. Jan Hus was a Czech hero of the Reformation, predating Martin Luther by a century, ending up burned at the stake for his protestations. There is the usual Protestant-Catholic divide in the Czech Republic, and these Hussite churches, Hus' spiritual descendants, bridge the divide, a Catholic sort of Protestantism.

After worship, the pastor invited me to lunch. His stories of life under Communism and of faith under Communism would turn any heart toward absolute commitment to freedom. He had wanted to be a pastor as a young man, but just when he was ordained the Communists took away the freedom to worship freely. He was not allowed to be a pastor, so he turned to a second love: art. He was a wood sculptor, often in the employ of the very Communists who prohibited the practice of his faith. "But," he told me proudly, "the Communists could not take God out of my hand, or out of my wood."

Maybe even my friend, Pissarro, couldn't get God out of his hands or his paint. Maybe I am connecting the dots for him. If I ever meet him, perhaps I will thank him and gently quote a sign I once saw, "It's all right if you don't believe in God. God believes in you."

Perhaps the mystery is in the creation, or The Creation. Christians have argued about creation to the point of silliness, and some have resolved it by simply emphasizing the very start of the Bible, "In the beginning God created." Or even simpler, "In the beginning God" (Genesis 1:1). Whenever and however creation takes place, in the beginning, God.

My journeys into art run the gamut. In North Adams there is the Massachusetts Museum of Contemporary Art, or "MASS MoCA." Housed in several acres of an abandoned factory, MASS MoCA has taken the art world by storm with a startling array of huge installation art. One building was filled by a haunting exhibit called "Izhar Patkin: The Wandering Veil" (2013-14).

Before I left, I re-read the lengthy introductory label that addressed this strange symbiotic relationship between atheism and faith, with neither one quite able to shake loose from the other.

The curator wrote: "There is nothing startling in this great work of art yet you are filled with a sense of bigness, grandeur, and the very conviction of truth. The veil is omnipresent in many cultures and religions, with the visible universe often understood as a veil that both hides and reveals God. Representation, abstraction, and manifestation come together."

Then, quoting the artist, "I am an atheist, I live in a secular world. My friend once challenged me to make a Shiva (a Hindu god). Regardless of my intention, sculpture gave way to manifestation. The statue is God, neither representation nor abstraction."

Whatever the theological merits of idols, the sculptor started out to make an inanimate sculpture only to end up making an animate god in the eyes of the believer. The artist's atheism couldn't stop the believer's beliefism. That actually is a compliment to both.

A New York Times review of an exhibit at New York's Metropolitan Museum of Art intrigued me. The exhibit was a collection of medieval treasures from Hildenshein, a town which had been a center of Christian activity one thousand years ago.

"Today its churches and museums still preserve one of the richest and densest concentrations of 11th century European religious art anywhere," wrote Holland Cotter in the review.[13] He went on to describe "one of the earliest fully-three dimensional sculptures known from medieval Europe... a five-foot-tall figure of the crucified Jesus."

What caught my attention was this personal comment: "The cross to which it was once attached is long gone, as is the paint that originally covered the body. But you don't miss them. Their absence throws attention more fully onto the details of carving and especially on the face, with its half-open, pain-drugged eyes and a pulled-down mouth that seems to express bitterness mixed with regret."

I can't speak for the reviewer. But he seems to be saying that you can take a carved Jesus off the cross, out of the church, let the paint chip away, stick him/it in a museum, and it still works. The reality of Jesus' death on the cross, the irony and the theology of that unique death, still come through. The final hours of Jesus' holy, wholly-lived life were filled with betrayal, denial, rejection, abandonment, agony, mockery and murder. A God-ordained murder, a God-abandoned victim, are perfectly depicted in the face of a now imperfect carving. Something transcended the ravages of time and taste so that the heart of Jesus speaks through the long-ago artist's skill. That is the power of faith and the power of art so intertwined as to be indistinguishable from one another.

Saint Zacchaeus

Long ago a church member complained that I used too many personal pronouns in my preaching and teaching: too much of *I*, *me*, and *my*.

---

[13] "Medieval Treasures from Hildenshein" .New York Times, September 20, 2013.

Guilty. I testify to what I know and give witness to what works for me. The painting that makes me probe deeper in faith may leave you cold. The books that inspire me to feel my faith intimately may bore you. The mountains in autumn that fill me with the presence of God may make you yearn for the ocean. But these are some of the things that work for me. They affirm my faith, strengthen it, inform it, push it.

There are infinite paths to faith in God. Someone like my father was born to it and never wavered from it. For some, there is a moment of conversion so dramatic you can never forget it, even if you wander off from time to time.

Others are convinced by others. There are people of faith in our lives we so admire that we know they would never steer us wrong, and we piggyback on their faith. Faith can be learned, adopted, inspired; simple or complex; mystical or practical. The point is that if it works it is inarguable. And if it does not work, it is inarguable.

The impetus for this chapter is three-fold. First, the popularity of atheism. Second, the power of art to move belief. Third, the writings of Tomáš Halík. If you care about atheism, or atheists, read Halík.

Father Halík is a Jesuit priest serving the academic community in Prague. His conversion is eerily similar to mine, a one-on-one dare to God to be real. During communism's heyday in Czechoslovakia, Halík served secretly as a priest. Now with the streets as free as the air, he devotes his work to seekers, especially to those who may not know they are seeking.

In his book *Patience With God,* a stunning and refreshing exploration of scripture, Halík delves into the story of Zacchaeus, Luke 19:1-10. Zacchaeus was a wealthy and corrupt tax collector serving the Romans, squeezing every bit of profit he could from fellow citizens. When Jesus passes through town, Zacchaeus, a small man, climbs a tree in order to observe the passing scene from a safe distance. Jesus spots him, calls out to him by name, and invites himself to dinner at Zacchaeus' home. The story ends with a celebratory Zacchaeus renouncing his old ways, promising restitution to everyone he cheated, and choosing to be a new person.

For Halík, Zacchaeus is the modern atheist, an outsider whether by his own choosing or by being pushed to the outside. Halík's life and ministry have been lived under the official, force-fed, crushing atheism of communism and the contemporary, willful atheistic apathy. Yet he refuses to see either type as a type, or as enemy or competition.

They are Zacchaeus. Cool and detached, yes. Above it all, removed, yes. Disliked and disrespected, yes. But susceptible to being known. It is instructive to Halík that Jesus calls Zacchaeus by name, and calls him to fellowship in his own home. He is not attacked or shamed. He is invited to be known, and to be true to himself. The seeker is sought, and loved, by name.

The Bible tells us that "Zacchaeus was seeking to see who Jesus was" (Luke 19:3). Nowhere in the story is Zacchaeus a fully formed believer. He does not acknowledge Jesus as the Christ, the Savior or even a prophet. But he was on the lookout for something, he was up in that tree for a reason, "to see who Jesus was."

Show me what you got, we might say. Or, what do you stand for... what are you to me?

Too often our approach is to be dismissive of those who dismiss us, to reject those who reject us, to keep at a distance those who choose to be distant from us.

Halík chooses to echo Jesus' Beatitudes, adding an extra one, "Blessed are the distant," and dares us to "warm that which is cold, moisten that which is dry... bring closer that which is distant".[14] Maybe Halík and I remember too clearly what it was like to think we were safely hiding in the tree, when all along we wanted someone, Someone, to call us by name.

Earlier I wrote that Inness' art states that paint is not just paint, a tree is not just a tree — there is always more. Halík takes that beyond his pulpit and his altar out into the streets of life where trees still embrace more Zacchaeuses than we dare to imagine.

We should see this as good news. Instead of fearing this phenomenon, be excited. Instead of fretting about everyone not in church, rejoice at all the people in trees who really do want to see who Jesus is. That, I know, is true.

This sounds like a lazy rationale for empty churches, offered by a leftist priest in our post-Christian world. Well, I have worshipped in Halík's church four times. On two Sunday nights I could not find a seat. On a Tuesday night there were two hundred at worship. At each service I felt like the oldest person there by decades. There is joy, excitement, intensity and faith in that ancient church that has faced, and withstood, all the evils of our times.

Bottom line? Atheism exists as much as God exists. Each requires Kierkegaard's "leap of faith" into the unknown. Whichever leap we take explains our worldview. We choose our worldview.

I choose to view the world and my life through the prism of faith. Everything else I can think of flows from that. Living with faith gives me a profound sense of sin and the equally profound "amazing grace" of forgiveness. That radically alters my attitude about myself and everybody else. Faith shapes my view of birth, death, everything in between, and what comes

---

[14] Halík, Tomáš, *Patience with God*. Doubleday, 2009. 11.

after. It breeds optimism, purpose, direction and determination. Priorities based on faith are startlingly different from what I would come up with on my own. Indeed, faith constantly confronts my every assumption, attitude, and behavior.

I choose to live my life with the assumption that someone is looking over my shoulder who really, really knows, and really, really cares. Yes, that can be awkward, embarrassing, frightening, intimidating. It can also be motivating, exciting and liberating.

One Sunday at Greenfield Hill Church we displayed a painting of Zacchaeus over the altar of our church. The artist captured that moment when Zacchaeus is released from the chains of greed and corruption and sin that have paralyzed his whole being. He has opened up his home and his life to Jesus, baring his wounds for all to see. Seated at the head of a sumptuous banquet, surrounded by family and friends who knew him at his worst, Zacchaeus is flinging bags of coins into the air. There is a euphoria about him as he is liberated from the sins of his day.

Zacchaeus had begun the day as an outcast, traitor, sinner, beyond the pale, beyond redemption, excluded. He ended the day in the Kingdom of God, loved, redeemed, forgiven, included. The bridge from the one to the other was Church, done right. At its best, Church outwits us at our worst:

> *He drew a circle that shut me out—*
> *Heretic, a rebel, a thing to flout.*
> *But Love and I had the wit to win:*
> *We drew a circle that took him in!*
>   *Edwin Markham, 'Outwitted'[15]*

---

[15] Markham, Edwin, (born Charles Edward Anson Markham April 23, 1852 – March 7, 1940). Epigram.

FIVE

Worship

Beer and pretzels for Holy Communion, I really did that. Not to mention peanut butter and jelly as the Eucharist, or apple juice and Goldfish crackers offered as The Lord's Supper.

I'm often amazed that I have made it this long as a pastor, having victimized trusting worshippers for decades with every passing fancy, trend, and whim.

During my first year in seminary, I was the Youth Pastor at Newton Highlands Congregational Church near my seminary in Newton Centre, Massachusetts. We held a high school youth retreat out on Cape Cod. I was as deep into 60's rock and folk music as you could get, and I remember using an album by "The Collectors" for much of the music and reflection. When it came time for Holy Communion I passed around beer and pretzels. Oh, sure, I had a theological/cultural rationale. I told the kids, and the surprisingly trusting adult chaperones, that when Jesus had his first Last Supper he used ubiquitous, readily available, not especially holy staples like bread and wine. I did not know much about the Passover roots of The Last Supper at that time. So the switch to ubiquitous, readily available, not especially holy staples like beer and pretzels seemed a perfectly plausible cultural transition from first century Jerusalem to 1968-ish suburban Boston.

That was my first step into Worship and Liturgy. At that point my career was a few weeks old, I had preached twice in my life, and never had organized a full worship service ever. Until then worship had been provided for me, fully packaged, delivered neatly in 60 minute segments. I knew what worship was: 4 hymns, a twenty-five minute sermon, choir, offering, call to worship, occasional communion, and benediction. Nothing much ever varied. The occasional Communion featured tiny pieces of white bread and little cups of Welch's Grape Juice, always Welch's.

Now, with the full grown arrogance of a first semester seminarian know it all, I served beer and pretzels to high school students for Holy Communion.

I first began to think about worship during my second year in seminary. By then I was "the seminarian" at The First Church of Bradford, Massachusetts. Along with traditional youth groups I was asked to help revitalize and expand worship at this historic, staid, comfortable, Congregational church. I agreed to start a new worship service to be held in the church's chapel and do it at 8:00 a.m. Different time, different place, different style. Out with the old, in with the

_____.

Exactly. A blank space.

I sat in my little office determined to break the boring shackles of ancient worship and create something stunning, startling, and revolutionary, yet worshipful. At the ripe old age of twenty-three I was prepared to toss out two thousand years of worship formula. What did they know? It was 1969, I was under thirty, and that was all the permission I needed.

But staring at that blank space humbled me. Maybe my father, with his 1950's worship formula, knew what he was doing. Maybe my worship professor at seminary knew what he was talking about when he forced me to study second century liturgy. Maybe old fashioned Catholicism and new-fangled Pentecostalism knew the basic elements of worship no matter how different the style.

Before long I had a fresh new worship as old as the hills. A Call to Worship to get things started, hymns to get people praising, prayers to talk to God, scripture to listen to God, preaching to make sense of it all, and offerings to say thank you to God. We didn't change what we did, just how we did it.

The offering was taken in a pressure cooker. The idea was that what we offer to God might reduce the pressure in the world. Somehow it made sense in 1969, plus my 1950's mother often produced wonderful Sunday dinners from her pressure cooker. Our music came from records played on a record player, from the Bee Gees (pre-disco) to Dylan, music and lyrics and messages that seemed pulled from the pages of the Bible. And yes, there was plenty of Bible, just presented in some way other than straight reading or standard standing-in-the-pulpit preaching.

Interestingly, I was inspired by the 1964 World's Fair. That World's Fair took place in my Queens backyard and one of its attractions was the Protestant Pavilion. That says something about Church right there. I was seventeen years old. The World's Fair was filled with futuristic displays, exotic world pavilions, and the New York Mets brand new stadium next door. Yet I was drawn repeatedly to the Protestant Pavilion.

Two presentations reminded me of the untapped power for worship. One was a short movie, *The Parable*, which presented the life and passion and resurrection of Jesus Christ in a provocative way, leaving audiences stunned, inspired, and knowing the story.

The Parable takes place in a travelling circus. In the opening scene a man applies white pancake make-up to his face, dresses all in white, gets on a donkey and follows the circus. Throughout the day this mysterious person intervenes to take on the burdens of various circus workers, taking their places, doing their work, giving them rest and affirmation. He carries water to the elephant, takes the place of a black man who is the dunk tank target. In the penultimate scene he enters the big tent where a violent human marionette skit is underway, complete with child abuse and wife abuse. The man in white lowers the human puppets, straps himself into the harness, is lifted up, and allows himself to be abused and killed by Magnus, the master puppeteer.

Throughout the film the only human sound is the haunting cry of agony as he dies. In an astounding conclusion, Magnus, the murderous puppeteer, is seen applying white pancake make-up to his face, and, dressed all in white, gets on his donkey and follows the circus.

That is good preaching and scripture and teaching in a short, experimental, avant-garde movie. It was truly worship-ful. The life of Christ, the parables of the Good Samaritan and the Wicked Tenants, Good Friday and Easter, and John 3:16 all put up on the screen, turning a corner of the World's Fair into Church.

The other World's Fair worship inspiration was the story of Job presented by an acting troupe all dressed in costumes that gave the illusion of stained glass. It left me knowing in detail the forty two chapters of an entire controversial book of the Bible. Again, good scripture and good preaching. One in a movie, one in a play.

Not surprisingly, I showed short movies and wrote little plays for our experimental church. In one play based on the story of Creation, I took the part of the snake, slithering down the aisle, no doubt leaving an indelible impression on a chapel filled with worshipers.

The filled chapel was a clear sign that people wanted Church. It was 8:00 a.m. in a church that had a hard time get-ting young people to come to church. Yet the Chapel was full of youth and parents. They wanted Church.

Twenty-five years later I found myself leading a "house church" in Americus, Georgia. My years as President of Habitat for Humanity, International led to my joining the Habitat headquarters staff and living in Americus. Over time a group of Habitat people, looking for a fresh and free-form style of worship, started gathering together informally.

For two years people filled our house for worship. With no budget, no bylaws, no name, no pastor, no churchy equipment like pews or pulpit, we were church. Week by week we recreated the experiments in worship of my seminary days, updated for the new world of the 90's, still using the elements of worship passed down from ancient worshipers and ancient places. Worship is still worship if it's worship. Church is still Church if it's Church. That is stating the obvious, but it is only obvious if it is intentional, if it connects the dots. Church is worship when it is intentional about connecting the dots.

In fact, Church may be essential to connecting the dots. Back in my college days anyone who went to church was met by good natured mockery based on interesting theology summarized as, "I don't need church. I can worship God in the backyard." True enough, but none of us ever worshipped God in the backyard, despite our best intentions. Church exists to take intentions and connect them to God. That's why it is called Organized Religion.

Yes, we are inspired by nature. By sunsets and mountains and rainbows, by snow and oceans and clouds, by music and quiet and thoughts, all manner of moments inspire us toward God. Church organizes those moments, connects those dots, and reinforces our faith by sharing it with others and seeing it in others.

I grew up in a neighborhood and at a time when religion was considered valuable, Church was popular, Christianity respected. Everyone went to Church or Synagogue. I didn't know anyone who didn't. Religion just was.

Entering the world of a New England prep school at age thirteen expanded my understanding. The Northfield–Mount Hermon School still had enough of D.L. Moody's old time religion that we had mandatory Church and mandatory religion classes. Quickly I learned both that Church was very important and that there was more to religion than just Church.

Taking a course on World Religions and reading *The Golden Bough* exploded my little religious brain. Suddenly I discovered that religion had roots and cause and journeys. Religion wasn't "just was." It was the result of intentional dot-connecting, from the primitive and mundane to the sophisticated and intellectual. People had actually thought stuff through. The Church I grew up in, the religion I accepted, were heir to millennia of thinking and practice, trial and error, as people sought to know God.

The religiosity I grew up taking for granted was anything but granted. We were part of the world's oldest tradition, making sense of the world around us. Our little corner church traced its roots back to the Pilgrims at Plymouth Rock, further back to Holland and England, a movement of people who only wanted the freedom to worship in their own way according to their own understanding. Some family gathered around a table in a country village in 16th century merry old England was not that different from a family in the merry old Fertile Crescent thousands of years before looking at life with wonder, awe, fear, and deciding, "I think we should...." Worship.

Yes, worship. At some point in human development people understood that much of life was beyond their control. Rain and harvest, birth and death, good and injustice, love and hate, these seemed to come from somewhere. The world must be more than chance; they began to think there may be some meaning beyond just being. Thinking and wondering leads to worship. For example, if you think the sun seems to help, you may want to thank the sun. Rain seems good, but not too much, so you may want to ask for the right balance. But whom to ask? And how? Thinking and wondering and questions lead to worship.

Each year, I do a couple of exercises with our Confirmation Class. Our confirmands are eighth graders trying to decide on their own whether God and Church and religion have any connection to them. Most of them were baptized as infants; they had no say in the beginnings of their religions life. Being confirmed is the first adult decision they make, a Congregationalist Bar Mitzvah. They decide to see the dots connected.

To help them make the connection I take them back to the days of disconnected dots. I ask them to imagine a world where nothing is known, a world before computers or books or TV. They are actually told the week before, "Your homework for next week is to forget everything you have ever known." At that next meeting the lights are turned off and they are invited to imagine the group of them sitting in a cave thousands of years ago. What do they talk about?

After some giggling and a bad joke or two they get into it. In a world before knowledge everything is a question, a challenge, a danger, a wonder, a dot.

"What's that big yellow thing up there? And where does it go when it's not there?"

"What's yellow? What's up? What's there?"

"Who is there?"

"Who are those people across the river?"

"Remember the one who went across the river and never came back?"

"We yelled to those people, and they yelled, but we couldn't understand."

"Where does rain come from?"

"Sometimes after lots of water everything is good, sometimes everything is gone! How do we get the right amount?"

"Remember that person from the cave that just stopped moving? When I touched him he fell over. Something was gone from him. Where did it go? Why?"

"Who is in charge?"

As the youngsters contribute to the discussion we soon find ourselves in the world of religion, even theology. In their imaginary cave they tire of being passive objects to which everything is done. They want a role to play. They see rain and sun, crops and fruit, life and death, war and peace, want and plenty. They recognize that someone other than their own group has power and influence over the events of daily life. They want to connect to that Someone.

It is a short skip and a jump to most of the activities connected with worship and Church. We want to know that "Someone," set apart with a capital "S" like Superman. We want that Someone to be on our side of the river, to help us. The kids suggest that maybe we should show fear, or respect, or leave offerings, or say "thanks." Maybe we should build a monument or a house for Someone. Maybe Someone needs something we have that we could give to show our respect?

This is a big thing. Whether for our confirmands or for ancient cave dwellers it is a big thing to begin thinking beyond one's own footprint in the universe, to think outside the cave. There is that moment in long ago history, as in our own lives, when we stop being passive recipients of the universe at work and want to engage those forces, or THE force, at work. In short, we want to know God, to understand and befriend God. We want God to help.

This is a big deal: when people have the humility to imagine a world and a way beyond their personal boundaries.

The words of Psalm 100 are frequently used to call congregations to worship. Of particular significance is the admission, "it is God that hath made us, and not we ourselves" (Psalm 110:3 KJV). That is why we worship. Once we recognize that we are not the sum and substance of the universe, we are not the be all and end all of creation, we are not the apple of our own eye, then we want to know more, experience more, and even dare to believe more.

That is the beginning of worship. Suddenly, the Book of Genesis, which means "beginning," makes sense. From Adam and Eve to Noah and the Ark, from the Tower of Babel to the Covenant with Abraham we see people trying to make sense of the world around them and the God who created it all. It is no wonder that Genesis 4 ends with, "at that time people began to call on the name of the Lord" (4:26). Inquiring minds want to know.

The ordering of that inquiring becomes the basis for worship and religion. During that one class "in the cave" we invite our Confirmands to come up with their own ideas of a god, of clergy, church, rituals, doctrines, theology – all out of their own imagination and wondering. They connect the dots between creation, Creator, and the created.

When we bring the Confirmands back to our world we discuss the young adult novel, *Godless* by Pete Hautman, a brilliant modern story about creating religion.[16] A group of Midwestern, small town teenagers are completely bored with sum-

---

[16] Hautman, Peter. *Godless*. Simon and Schuster. 2005.

mer. Nothing to do, nowhere to go, they don't much like their parents and definitely don't like their parents' religion. The best rebellion they can imagine is to start their own religion.

Much like my 1960's experiment with creating contemporary worship began by starting with a blank slate, these young people, too, start with nothing and end up quite conventional, creating both church and worship.

They start with the most basic theological question: what is most important? Even their teenage satirical atheism understands the Biblical idea that whatever is most important to you is your god. Money, sex, power, work, passions all vie with named and nameless, popular and forgotten, divinities.

The teenagers in *Godless* choose water as most important. In a lot of small towns the tallest building is the water tower, so that is their church. In short order they decide all the crucial issues of classic church and classic worship. Who is in, who is out? Who leads, who follows? What is required, what is forbidden? How do you join, how do you get expelled? What are the blessings and curses, rewards and punishments? What must you do to truly connect with water? What are the consequences?

Taken together, those two exercises result in basic religion. Put it into practice, you've got worship. In two short weeks our youth go from Neanderthal cave theology to creating their own church. Imagine, then, that you came to Greenfield Hill Congregational Church on a Sunday morning. How far removed are we from folks leaving an offering at the foot of a gnarled baobab tree, or beginning the morning with folded hands facing the sun, or humbly bowing down five times a day toward Mecca, or dancing ecstatically to the Pentecostal sounds of speaking in tongues, or adrift on clouds of incense before a life size crucifix in a Serbian Orthodox

Church in Belgrade? These are the halting, human steps toward worship.

The Bible gives some basics for worship, even allowing for changes over time. God ordains the idea of Sabbath rest right at the beginning by providing divine example. God rests.

By the seventh day God had finished the work he had been doing; so on the seventh day God rested from all the work. And God blessed the seventh day and made it holy because on it God rested from all the work of creating.

(Genesis 2: 2-3)

In case anyone did not get the message, God made it law in The Ten Commandments, "Remember the Sabbath day by keeping it holy. Six days you shall labor and do all your work, but the seventh is a Sabbath to the Lord your God" (Exodus 20: 8-9). Eventually, worship became the key activity on the Sabbath, which is how we ended up with the old Blue Laws. Those laws, popular in New England, restricted what could be bought or done on the Sabbath. The goal was to clear the schedule for Church.

By then the Sabbath, following Christian custom, had been switched from Saturday to Sunday. Nevertheless, the goal remained the same, to use one day a week not only for rest but also for concentrating on God. Worship became the method, the vehicle for concentration.

I was ordained at the First Baptist Church of Haverhill, Massachusetts, in 1971. That church provided what would be my last experience of the old fashioned way of Sunday Church life.

We began with a Sunday school that involved most of the whole Church, it was not just for children. The big worship service later in the morning was often followed by adult classes, special events, lunches. Youth ministry filled the afternoons before evening worship completed the "day of rest." In other words, the day of rest was transformed into a day of Church.

In today's world, or certainly my northeast, New England, American corner of today's world, Church has to compete mightily for people's attention, time, or involvement. The Sabbath day of rest, if it ever existed, has been replaced by a day of frenetic, hectic activity. Youth sports dominate family life. Today's young athletes play more games, with more practices, more travel, more full day or two day tournaments. The competition for fields or ice time means earlier games and later games. Even sports team fundraisers and end of year award banquets take place on Sunday mornings.

Sports are only part of the mix that squeezes worship out of Sunday priorities. Add in cultural activities, family events, town and charity based festivals and fundraisers, and the demands on everyone's time are crazy. When someone actually gets a completely free Sunday it is no wonder they might choose to skip Church.

Yet the yearning for true worship remains strong. There is still a universal desire to know and to be known by God. People pursue that yearning in different ways, or if they don't purse it they still miss it. People want to worship.

My math may be wrong but it seems like there are a hundred success stories out there for every failure, and somehow at the same time there are a hundred failures for every success story as churches try to attract and keep worshippers. I read of a new church start-up that chose to have its main worship at 5:00 p.m. on Sundays in order to allow people to do all those other Sunday activities without guilt. Churches are renting theaters, rock 'n' roll venues, and cafes in order to take advantage of everything from comfortable seating and ample parking to ambience and cache. My 1960's idea of using drama and film is now trendy. Jazz bands, mini orchestras, rock groups lead the singing.

People want to know God, want to worship, want to be inspired, want to be together, all the elements of basic Church on a Sunday. To accomplish these mutual goals we need to rethink, maybe reconfigure, time, space, style, our whole delivery system. It should be comforting, even invigorating, to know that people want what Church has.

Greenfield Hill Congregational Church is not a rock 'n' roll venue with comfortable seating and ample parking. Whatever you think a historic New England Congregational Church should look like, that is Greenfield Hill. A small, simple, plain, almost square white clapboard Church, sitting on the same place since 1725, and folks have come there each Sunday to end one week and begin another. It is where we do Church.

There is nothing about us that is fancy on a Sunday morning. A couple of hymns, some Bible readings, a not too long sermon, a little music, prayers here and there, an offering. We can get you in and out in under an hour.

But magic happens there. Magic is when something happens that is obvious yet you can't explain it. Buffy St. Marie, legendary folk singer, sang, "God is alive, magic is afoot," and that is as good an explanation as can be provided. If God is alive and people are open and expectant you have the key ingredients for worship.

Rick Warren, popular mega-Church pastor, confesses in his book, *The Purpose Driven Church*, that he gets annoyed when he hears someone complain, "I don't get anything out of Church." He wants to ask them, "Well, what did you bring to church?"[17] In short, if you can get people to Church, and if the

---

[17] Warren, Rick. *The Purpose Driven Church.* Zondervan, 1995.

people bring something to Church, and if God is alive, then magic is afoot.

What to bring? The Bible's prescription for good worship can be summarized as attitude and expectation. The attitude is gratitude, and the expectation is for a changed and challenged life. Early on, worship was mostly about tangible offerings and bloody sacrifices, gifts to God that would show remorse for sins and thanks for blessings. But the overemphasis on material things as proof of piety got rejected long before New Testament Christianity. The prophet Amos reported God's disgust this way:

> *I hate, I despise your religious feasts;*
> *I cannot stand your assemblies.*
> *Even though you bring me offerings,*
> *I will not accept them ...*
> *Away with the noise of your songs!*
> *I will not listen to the music.*　　　　(Amos 5:21-23)

A pastor of the Old First Church of Jerusalem might be led to ask God, "okay, but other than *that,* how did you enjoy the service?!" God clearly was not pleased with the state of worship in ancient Israel. They had all the rituals and traditions, the pageantry, the ins and outs of religious regulations. The teenagers in *Godless* would have been right at home. But God was not pleased. That worship left God empty.

So what does God want? According to Amos, "let justice roll down like waters, and righteousness like an ever-flowing stream" (Amos 5: 24). That is the change and challenge that goes along with the attitude of gratitude. It begins with wanting worship and its results. God wants us to want to be there. "I love the house where you live, O Lord," sings the Psalmist (Psalm 26:8). "One thing I ask, that I may dwell in the house of the Lord all my days, to gaze upon the beauty of the Lord and to seek God in God's temple" (Psalm 27:4).

Worship is meant to be a great experience! The Bible speaks of beauty, love, splendor and holiness all wrapped together in worship.

But not as an end in itself. In worship we encounter God in order to be prepared to encounter the world.

Amos' spiritual twin, Micah, considers the act of worship, asks a key question and then provides a seminal answer. He begins, "with what shall I come before the Lord, and bow down before God?" (Micah 6:6).

We come into Church, we see the cross on the altar, the words on the hymn page. We hear "the word of the Lord" pronounced and exhorted. There is an aura to the place fed by memories and needs and the very place itself. We got up that morning and chose to do Church. We are ready to "come before the Lord and bow down," to show worship. What is God's expectation? Micah continues, bluntly:

> He has told you, O mortal, what is good;
> and what does the Lord require of you
> but to do justice, and to love kindness,
> and to walk humbly with your God?
>
> (Micah 6:8, NRSV)

Worship starts with love and ends with determination. We come with joy looking for a break from the world, a literal Sabbath. An hour or so later we leave renewed, reinvigorated to face the very same world that beat us down the week before. Worship keeps us in the game. In the process we participate in traditions and rituals, some of which we don't understand or like, we give some money to keep Church going, we see old friends and meet new people, we sign up to do something that needs doing, we shake a few hands, we go home.

If done right we walk out with heads up, chest out, shoulders straight, a feisty step in our walk. Watch out, world. An energy devoted to justice and righteousness AND to love and humility is about to be unleashed. That little conjunction, "and," is crucial. Too much religion down through the ages and currently claims to be on the side of justice and righteousness, while beheading and torturing, burning at the stake and inquisitioning, enslaving and oppressing. It is impossible to be humble and loving while being atrociously brutal at the same time. God's demand to be humble and merciful is meant as a check on our indignant desire to do justice. Indignation with humility and mercy will always be different than indignation with arrogance. Church is meant to keep that righteous balance.

St. Paul had that balance. To the Romans he wrote, "Therefore, I urge you to offer your bodies as living sacrifices, holy and pleasing to God. This is your spiritual act of worship" (Romans 12:1). Taken all together this is a design for worship. We are God's best offering. We offer ourselves to God, God offers us to the world. Both parts of the exchange are done with love and humility. The end result is that God is known, we are loved, the world is challenged.

Worship is that moment, that experience, where we give ourselves over to God. That kind of concentration at anything is increasingly rare. When you go to Broadway or the movie theater you go with anticipation and expectation, you pay your money, you choose your seat carefully, you have prepared ahead of time. Then, before it starts, they demand that you pay attention. We are told to turn off our cell phones, to deactivate anything that would distract you or others. The Broadway cast and the movie stars want you to give yourselves over to them for two hours. In return they promise you their best.

Worship is the same deal. Your best and God's best join together.

I have been blessed. From the earliest days of my career I have been given tremendous freedom to do Church in any way I want. When it comes to worship that has meant that on most Sunday mornings I have stayed close to my church's traditions, delivering a worship experience in tune with their expectations. The faithfulness to their needs earns me the right to inject changes here and there. My experience is that people will try most anything if, first, it is done well, and second, if they know that the normal will return.

Away from Sunday morning I have been free to try anything, and we have. Jazz worship, modern dance, Taizé meditation, plays and musicals, guest choirs and speakers, dinner worship. We have tried worship that was longer or shorter, louder or softer.

Truth is, some experiments have worked, some haven't. We tried an outdoor summer service at dusk; it took weeks for us to realize that any service at which there were more mosquitoes in attendance than people was no fun for anyone. And for years, we held a monthly Saturday evening service. If the service included a special event, like a choir or a Christian acting troupe, attendance could be 150; without that, we might get three. Sometimes just me and Alida. It became obvious, in the case of those services, that we were trying to create a demand for something no one was demanding: Saturday night worship. We were programming and entertaining, but not worshiping.

Nevertheless, I remained struck by two realities. One, people really did want to worship. Two, people are finding it more and more complicated to worship on Sunday mornings. There are more and more long holiday weekends, more and more Sunday morning conflicts. People's absence from the pews is not a reflection of their unbelief or laziness or apathy; it's the result of changing societal values and personal priorities. Society does not value Church or Sunday mornings the way it once did. At the same time people place more value than ever on family time, leisure, sports.

So, yes, people still want to worship but often worship does not fit their schedule. Should I whine or try guilt? No, thank you. I hate whining, I love the bar sign that threatens: "$5 Fine for Whining." As for guilt, religion has used that for thousands of years. Anything that is done forever loses its impact. I would bet that half the people who joined our church in the past decade said that they had grown tired of the guilt they got elsewhere. So, no, I am not going to tell a mom to tell her son, "You can't play in your Little League game because you must come to Church." Nor am I going to tell the mom to skip the game so that at least someone from the family will be in church.

This actually is not that new a phenomenon. I was about fifteen when my baseball playing days began requiring Sunday morning games, a major shock to my Sabbath observing family and Church. We really kept the Sabbath. This meant no Sunday newspaper, little T.V., mostly quiet games inside or out.

The Deacons and my father agreed to write to the respected editor of a major Christian magazine, and to abide by his decision. He must have loved baseball because his King Solomon-like declaration was that a boy could be doing a lot worse things on a Sunday morning than playing baseball. Therefore, he decreed, I should be permitted to play baseball, with two requirements. First, I should not argue with the umpire on the Sabbath. Second, I should find a Church with a Sunday evening service and get there for worship. I did. That was my 1960's New York City Church family adjustment to changing social realities and personal priorities. We were a Church-loving, baseball crazy family that found a way to accommodate both.

At Greenfield Hill Church we have succeeded with two experiments in worship worth mentioning. One is an early Sunday morning summer service, outdoors. The other is a Sunday evening worship done every three months. For twenty years we have done the outdoor worship under a large shade tree for the twelve weeks of summer. Each worship is led by church members, each is entirely different. They are creative, fun, informal, interactive. Above all, they are successful worship by every measure: God's, the pastors', and the congregation's. The people who lead put a lot of thought into it, some starting months ahead to prepare. Topics are substantive and provocative, tackling everything from the Trinity to Thomas Jefferson's critique of the Bible and Christianity, from life's changes to the power of prayer. Being outdoors makes it comfortable for drinking coffee, eating a donut, easy discussion, and allowing children to roam when they get restless.

The popularity of this lay-led worship is evident not only in the attendance, but in the eagerness with which church members sign up to lead one of the services. In the early years, the pastors often had to cover several open Sundays; now we have a waiting list of lay leaders. Early on, the perception was that these services were "worship lite" — but no more. With all the elements of worship, with all the purpose of worship, this is true worship. People, we have found, want to worship, and not always indoors for an hour led by the pastor.

"Sports Worship" is another evolving success in alternative worship. I am not ready to bottle it yet for mass distribution, but it has a lot of pieces that show promise. One year a superb high school basketball player told us that we shouldn't take it personally that sports-active teenagers like her didn't come to Sunday morning Church. With endless pressures and activities all week long, Sunday mornings, she explained, were the only time to sleep late.

This high school athlete had given me the best clue for a new 'hook' to worship: athletics. Sports were her life. To squeeze worship into her life the obvious channel was sports.

Sports Worship is the result – and the time we've settled on is Sunday evenings. In America at large, and certainly in our town, sports dominate life. Kids have games and practices, parents do the driving and cheering, siblings are along for the ride. Adults are also playing. With six golf courses within a ten minute ride, and the ocean nearby, our people are immersed in sailing, golf tournaments, tennis, running, cycling. You name it and someone is doing it competitively and regularly from five-year-olds to ninety-year-olds.

Complaining about it is boring, counterproductive and small minded. With Sports Worship we embrace the world of sports as a ready-made platform for worship. We create a worship experience out of the world of sports, and we populate the service with middle school and high school athletes. We have had two wrestlers read the scriptures, three volleyball players share the prayer, six Little Leaguers be the ushers, all of our lacrosse players be the message.

For the message, I interview people whose sports experiences mirror the experiences and lessons of faith. My questions get to the heart of the connection between faith and daily life, and to what it takes to do your best, to learn, to grow, to succeed. Coaches, former college football and lacrosse players, All American soccer and water polo players, world-class sailors, champion body builders and swimmers have had a turn. We use the same interview format with high school athletes, probing them for what they have learned and how they apply it to daily life.

Within minutes of the very first Sports Worship we knew we had hit a home run. With a huge crowd of youngsters dragged to Church on a Sunday night by hopeful parents, an

85-year-old legendary high school basketball coach climbed slowly to the pulpit, and stole the show. He talked about faith and family, the importance of practice and perseverance, the role of Church, of teamwork.

Every Sports Worship has echoed a basic message, whether prepared or spontaneous, coach or player, adult or child. The best of sports, the best of family life, the best of business, the best of Church rests on a common formula. Patience, prayer, not giving up, mutual respect, courage, perspective, focus, a sense of calling, an awareness of gifts, a desire to do your best, these are all attributes that fuel us on the playing field and in the Church pew, in the classroom and the living room and the boardroom.

Whether it is Rick Warren asking "What do you bring to Church?", or a state champion football coach declaring that he only wants "players who will love one another as much as they love themselves," or a high school three-sport star stating emphatically that only Jesus stands by him in defeat and failure as well as triumph and glory, there is an undeniable echo from the world of sports into faith and daily life.

One of our Deacons told of playing college football in the largest come from behind victory in NCAA Division 1 history. Behind 35-0 at halftime in an away game, they fought back to victory. You can't help but wonder what went on on the side-lines during the first half, in the locker room at halftime, in the trenches during the second half. What had they picked up, and from where, that they didn't just quit?

Every person at Sports Worship that night knew what it was like to be behind 35-0 at halftime, and still have to play. The mother with a cancer diagnosis, the dad who just lost his job, the family whose mortgage was way behind, the young athletes whose dreams of playing have been derailed by being cut or benched or injured, the high school junior who just now has decided to get serious about school, the parents with a child in deep trouble, the business person facing bankruptcy – we have all been way behind, staring defeat in the face.

Just about every person who has spoken at Sports Worship has touched upon how to face adversity, loss, failure, disappointment and still find the resolve to continue, to prosper, to excel, to stay in the game of life and of faith.

Sports provide ready-made and readily understood parables, as simple as the ones Jesus told. Jesus' parables of The Good Samaritan, The Prodigal Son, the Sower, and the Lost Sheep all drew upon daily life. None of those parables are overtly religious in and of themselves. But they provided material that Jesus used to explore the path to deeper faith. That, after all, is a key desire of worship. All of us come to Church in a certain state, a certain frame of mind. We hope to emerge an hour later in a better state, a better frame of mind.

I once had a wonderful Deacon in my Church who was a successful Madison Avenue advertising executive. He told me, "David, there are a lot of people who get paid a lot more money than you do to make my life miserable. People on the subway, people at work, clients. And they are good at it. So when I come to Church I need to go out feeling better than I did when I came in."

That was a huge revelation to me about worship. Early in my career I was a great haranguer. I could beat people up a dozen ways in a Sunday service, trying to make them feel guilty. It could be the Vietnam War, nuclear disarmament, poverty, greed, racism, I could take any topic and use it as a cudgel to force good people into being what I thought they should be. Of course, I called it being "prophetic," but mostly I was just a nag. My "Mad Man" Deacon friend had a higher view of worship. After being nagged and harangued all week long by people who were real pros at it, he didn't need it from an amateur like me. He came to Church for something better, truer, more lasting.

We come to worship to know God. And if the Bible is true that "God is love." (1 John 4:8), then Love is what we ought to experience in worship. If we do experience God's love then we have truly worshipped, and we will go out feeling better than when we came in. No wonder the Psalm writers could declare, "I was glad when they said unto me, 'let us go in to the house of Lord to worship'" (Psalm 122:1). "I would rather be a door-keeper in the house of the Lord than anything else" (Psalm 84:10). Those folks couldn't wait to get to Church. Something was happening there that made them glad, something that struck them as being better than anything else they could be doing.

Perhaps we miss the point when we talk about Jesus chasing the money changers out of the temple (Matthew 21:12-13). I admit, I have usually focused on this as a rare example of Jesus being angry. I enjoy presenting the spectacle of Jesus, whip in hand, tossing chairs around, overturning tables, setting free the array of penned up sacrificial animals, maybe kicking a few vendors in the seat of the pants. Hooray for righteous indignation!

But preachers like me overlook Jesus' real purpose. He reminded everyone of the role of worship, "my house shall be a house of prayer." Prayer is conversation with God, conversation is interaction and intimacy, this is how we get to know one another on a deeper level. In worship we invite one another and God to enter into a time of intimacy. Jesus was simply clearing the clutter so folks could enjoy worship and be glad to be there. That is Church.

SIX

All Scripture is Profitable:
My Love Affair with the Bible

The Bible tells us, "all scripture is profitable" (2nd Timothy 3:16). I agree, but some scriptures make us cringe. Even this verse goes on to remind us that, among its several purposes, scripture is profitable for "reproof and rebuke." We may look to the Bible to be inspired and instructed, but back away at being reproofed and rebuked.

My love affair with the Bible began in earnest on that boardwalk in Coney Island when I was giving away free scriptures. I felt first hand its power to inspire and rebuke. The folks who hugged me had found inspiration and strength in the Bible; the folks who assaulted me had no doubt been reproofed and rebuked by someone quoting the Bible. My huggers and assaulters both offered convincing proof that the Bible was powerful, and that I needed to take it seriously.

Down deep I knew that, but had lost track of it. I was raised with the Bible, went to a terrific Sunday School with old fashioned memorization and new fashioned comic books teaching us scripture. My father's Vacation Bible School was an extravaganza of Bible fun that drew the whole neighborhood. My prep school years included mandatory Bible classes with superb teachers. The Bible was not a dusty, arcane relic sitting on a shelf.

Nevertheless, as President Bush the younger admitted, "When I was young and foolish I was young and foolish" ... and I did not take the Bible seriously.

The world takes the Bible seriously. Listen to the Rolling Stones' "Prodigal Son"; see Archibald MacLeish's play about

Job, "J.B."; read John Bunyan's classic "Pilgrim's Progress"; watch Mel Gibson's "The Passion of the Christ" or Russell Crowe's "Noah"; remember the Broadway musicals "Jesus Christ, Superstar" and "Godspell"; read Flannery O'Connor's short stories; look at art work in museums; listen to politicians' rhetoric; pick up countless novels; watch TV. Everywhere people are operating from the same premise: this scripture is profitable, let's see what we can do with it.

Truth is, it works, sometimes as iron, sometimes as irony.

The popular TV lawyer show, "The Good Wife," had a fascinating episode in which the two opposing clients force their lawyers to agree to binding arbitration through a Christian pastor. Within moments the prosecutor and the defense attorney are throwing Bible verses at each other, trying to out-scripture one another. The Bible is ripe for abuse and exploitation and it has been ever thus. When Jesus was in the wilderness the Devil quoted scripture to win Jesus over. Both sides of the Civil War resorted to scripture to oppose or to favor slavery. The Bible has been a tool for good and ill because it works, it has clout, influence, power, authority. That's why people grab for the Bible when they want to make a good point.

Jesus, whose words became scripture, was said to have spoken "as one with authority" (Matthew 7:29). That authority came from within. No outside entity validated him. The widely-read mini-biography of Jesus, *One Solitary Life*, highlights Jesus' lack of credentials. It reminds us that he had no degrees, no politics, no military, no platform. Jesus just was, or is, and that was, or is, enough.[18]

---

[18] *One Solitary Life* is attributed to James Alan Francis, from a 1926 sermon to the Baptist Young People's Union

Likewise, the Bible's authority is itself. We pick it up, we read it, we apply it, it works. Or it doesn't. Someone's opinion of it is often that simple.

One Christmas my grandparents gave me a little wooden box. Inside were tiny scrolls, each with a Bible verse written on it, and a little spindle to pick one out each day. That was the idea, to start every day by choosing a scroll at random. The beauty of it was its simplicity. A tiny spindle picking out a tiny scroll with a tiny verse printed in tiny print, creating a grandeur belying its simplicity. Each verse was carefully chosen to provide a perfect boost of whatever, maybe faith, maybe confidence, maybe hope, maybe encouragement. In its almost naïve simplicity it worked.

Nothing works more perfectly than the 23rd Psalm. Many of my funerals begin with a phone call from a funeral director who informs me that the deceased's family has no church, and they don't want any religious stuff in the service. But would I please include the 23rd Psalm? When I meet with the family I usually hear about some mean pastor or rude church or silly rules that put them off religion for good. Then, as we go through Psalm 23, they are reopened to the world of faith. The family wasn't anti-scripture or anti-faith, just anti-whatever some religion or pastor had done to them.

Scripture at its best opens us up, making it all profitable, including the ones that offer reproof or rebuke, or make us cringe. My whole approach to the Bible is that there is a reason each verse is in there, good, bad, or ugly, so deal with it. Jacob got points for trying to wrestle God to the ground and pin him down, literally, so why not try it ourselves? (Genesis 32: 24-28).

I came of spiritual age at a time when Protestant Christianity was doing a good job of looking at scripture critically. 'Critically' in this context does not mean critiquing, dismissing or correcting scripture; it refers to looking closely at texts, and examining their contexts in order to deepen appreciation. Seminary introduced me to all sorts of Biblical criticism – form criticism, historical criticism, redaction criticism – all 20th-century scholarly attempts to help the reader understand the origins and meaning of scriptural texts more fully. To say that all scripture is profitable, or to call oneself a Bible-believing Christian, or to believe that the Bible is inspired, does not require wearing blinders or putting one's head in the sand. The Bible is strong enough to stand up to critical scrutiny. I know the verses about killing your disobedient son, women keeping silent in church, slaughtering old people, and snake handling. For a verse to be profitable does not mean it is agreeable. Thomas Jefferson is said to have used his scissors to cut out the parts he didn't like. I would rather face them head on, wrestle them to the ground.

God gives us a head to use. These scriptures have been around for thousands of years, shaping the thinking and behavior and faith of amazing people, some amazingly good and some amazingly bad. Using our head, we can profit even from the scriptures that make us scratch our heads.

One obvious example of head-scratching scripture is Genesis 22. Prior to this chapter, Abraham and Sarah have courageously stepped out in faith to accept God's invitation to start a new people. Their agreement with God —Abraham's covenant — was that they would offer their faith to God, and in return God would offer blessings to their descendants. By Chapter 21 Abraham and Sarah are deep into old age, but with no kids, no heirs, no descendants to inherit God's promised blessings. Miraculously, the elderly Sarah then has a baby, Isaac, the apple of their eyes, their heart's desire, their answered prayer.

Then, to our horror, in Chapter 22, God tells Abraham to sacrifice Isaac, and Abraham agrees. He builds an altar, places his son on it, and, with a knife clutched in his fist, raises his hand to kill his own child at God's command.

What is going on here? Some modern thinkers call this child abuse, ancient barbarism at the least. Yes, but Abraham does stop in mid-thrust, halted by an angel. Seeing a ram caught in a thicket, Abraham sacrifices the ram instead. God then proceeds to bless Abraham profusely with a revitalized covenant, and Abraham lives on in sacred memory, forever credited with blind faith obedience (Genesis 22: 15-18). No blood, no foul.

Dare we think a bit harder on that one? Dare we use our own head, our reason, a little amateur psychology into the mind of God? Why not! I see God drawing out this slow-building, disturbing story in order to dramatize the "NO!", not the willingness to almost. This scripture really is profitable to reproof and rebuke the religious history of human sacrifice. Slaves, virgins, children, captured innocents have been sacrificed the world over to appease some idea of a blood thirsty God.

There are plenty of lessons in Abraham's story, lots of entry points for good discussions about faith and blind faith, obedience, patience, even contemporary politics in the Middle East. But let me add one more entry point. I believe God chose such a dramatic turn of events to stop horror in its tracks in a way that would never be forgotten.

The Bible invites us to dig deep, think hard, make use. The stories that puzzle us the most invite the deepest digging. Biblically speaking, that's where the real work of faith takes place. When Jesus says we should be nice to kids, that's not much of a strain (Mark 9:36-37; 10:13-14). When he washes his disciples' feet, and tells us to do the same, he is pushing the envelope a bit (John 13: 12-17). When he befriends enemies and traitors, physical and social lepers, it starts to get very uncomfortable. Toss in miracles, demons, the supernatural and the just plain impossible, we are in tough territory. When the Bible pushes the envelope, makes us uncomfortable, and tosses in the impossible, that's when the fun begins.

I write a lot of poetry, mostly based on scriptures. It began with the frenzy accompanying the year 2000. People were coming up with lists of the greatest one hundred novels of the 20th century, the top one hundred movies, songs, events, athletes. That spurred me to write a poem for each of the 100 most important scriptures, more daunting than I imagined. It soon expanded from verses to persons, places, stories, events, all taken from scripture.

The process was a microcosm of this chapter. To write each poem I had to start with the premise that it was serious stuff, it deserved my best effort, it was important, it was profitable — that is, it was worth it.

Then I had to reason with it. Read it, look at it, turn it inside out, study it, and pray about it. As I did with the Inness paintings, I would ask over and over again, "What are you saying to me? What do you want me to know?" The more I wrote the more I wanted to tackle the tough stuff.

In one poem, "Something Happened That Day," I tackled the miracles that make skeptics so skeptical and ask us, "how can you believe such a thing?!" My answer is that in each instance *something* must have happened that day that made folks pause and wonder, and believe. I don't think St. John's publisher told him that his first draft of his Gospel needed some pizzazz and suggested he add a story in which there's a guy who's been dead for days, to the point that the corpse has begun to stink — and then have Jesus show up and raise Lazarus from the dead (John 11). Nor do I think that the disciples made up stories out of whole cloth about Jesus calming a storm or healing a paralytic or feeding five thousand people with five loaves of bread and two fish. Something happened that day that left an impact so great that those same witnesses and writers sacrificed everything, including their lives, to tell the world.

Something Happened That Day
(Matthew 14:22-33)

Something happened that day
some wondrous surprise
that defies
the explanation
of mind or eyes
something beyond belief
but there it is
to be believed.

Something happened that day
some imagined possibility
brought concrete reality to its knees
Something unknowable got known
Something undoable got done
something peculiar
made folks remember
something "passing strange"
as they used to say
happened that day
Something outside the normal range
of whatever
human endeavor
finds acceptable.

Lazarus raised from the dead
thousands fed
with little fish

and too little bread ...
Something happened that day.

Some spoken word
some inner thought
some outward touch
a leper made clean
a woman redeemed
Legion set free
a blind man could see
all would say
Something happened that day
Something came their way
A whisper of the Spirit wind
A little miracle within.

From birth in Bethlehem to victory in Jerusalem
and everything in between
calming troubled waters on the sea
walking on water in Galilee
it cannot be explained away
Something happened that day.

Nero's torches
Japanese crosses
Roman Coliseum
and tyrant's prison
tempted folks to weigh
carefully
whether something happened that day.

But something persevered
something rang true
something could not be denied

something that could not happen
happened some way that day
Something
took breath and doubt away.
Something
happened
that day.[19]

Faith and the Bible go hand in hand. The Bible says correctly, "Faith is being sure of what we hope for, and certain of what we cannot see" (Hebrews 11:1). In the therapeutic world people say, "Give yourself permission to ..." before risking more than you thought possible. In planning meetings, the leader, to get things going, will announce, "I've set the permission meter at 100," meaning anything goes. In effect, through faith we give the Bible permission to speak with authority. We give permission to ourselves to take seriously the unlikely, the unbelievable, from the Easter resurrection to "blessed are they that mourn," from Jesus walking on water to "love your enemies." It is faith that imbues scripture with power, which compels us to dig deep especially when verses trouble us.

Jesus was a nice guy. That is universally accepted. Even those who do not accept his divinity, who disagree with his teachings, who oppose his religion and politics, who reject his miracles, who can't stand his Church, they still agree that he was a nice guy. When we come up against scriptures that show him being not nice it is troubling.

Now, some people welcome a harsh Christ. It supports their image of Jesus returning to earth on a white horse at the

---

[19] Rowe, David Johnson. *"Something Happened that Day."* In *Fieldstones of Faith, Vol. II.* Lulu Press, 2011.

"end times" to send most of the world to hell. When Jesus kills an unproductive fig tree (Mark 11:12-14, 20-21), assaults the money changers in the Temple (Mark 11:15-17), boasts that he came not to bring peace but a sword (Matthew 10:34), or is just plain cruel, that fits their Jesus created in their own image.

It reminds me of a poem by William Blake. Blake was a visionary, mystical, hypercritical, super-spiritual, brilliant polymath whom I would dearly love to have met but who might have been a tough dinner companion. In his wonderfully meandering "The Everlasting Gospel," Blake writes:

> *"The vision of Christ that thou dost see*
> *Is my vision's greatest enemy ...*
> *Thine loves the same world mine hates*
> *Thy heaven doors are my Hell gates ...*
> *Both read the Bible day and night*
> *But thou readst black where I read white"*[20]

Or, to be more blunt, my Jesus ain't your Jesus. Maybe it is true that we all get the Jesus we want, or need. I want, need Jesus to be a nice guy. But what to do when I come up against a tough verse that unsettles my nice image of Jesus, or any other tough verse? I do two things. First, I look at it in the larger context of all we know about Jesus. Second, I wrestle it to the ground and demand, "what are you saying to me?"

Matthew 15 and Mark 7 tell an awful story about Jesus. It is rude, prejudiced, and ugly. Jesus and the disciples were visiting a distinctly non-Jewish area when their peace was disturbed by a frantic, demanding mother. Her daughter was "suffering terribly from demon-possession" and begged for

---

[20] Blake, William. *The Complete Poems*. Longman, 1971, p. 850.

help (Matthew 15:22). Jesus' reply takes our breath away. "I was sent only to the lost sheep of Israel. It is not right to take the children's bread and toss it to their dogs" (vs. 24-26).

Two thousand years of preachers have tried to get Jesus off the hook for this one, defending his single-minded focus on Jews, or explaining that he was testing the woman's faith, or maybe he was just plum tuckered out. No matter how you cut it, this is a bad scene. Referring to this non-Israelite, non-Jewish, Canaanite, Phoenician, worried mother as a "dog" is inexcusable.

So I don't excuse it. The verse is in the Bible, it is not nice, it does not show Jesus in a good light. But if all scripture is profitable, what is the profit here? The woman's faith and persistence are commendable. Jesus' change of heart is instructive. Thank God for the nice miracle at the end. I get all that.

I still want to wrestle it some more. In my poem, "God's Dog," I don't disavow the scripture, or soften it, or rationalize it. It is there, in all its stark reality. The poem looks at that profitable scripture and stark reality from the "dog's" perspective.

God's Dog
(Mark 7:25-30)

He called me a dog.
People say
dog
is God
spelled backwards
then pause
like that's so deep
some fathomable mystery
to soften my misery

but it hurts
I don't care what higher purpose
lurks
beneath the curse
it hurts
to be called
a dog,
by God

but I do not yield
this dog will not be heeled
by God or anyone
I surprise myself, and him
I claw my way back
to human
my bark is sharp
"I am able"
said I to the Master
"to eat crumbs from your table." [21]

This is also where the larger context comes in, reminding us not to "proof text." Proof texting is when you take one verse out of context to prove your point. For example: the Bible mentions slaves, so slavery must be okay. Paul handled a snake, so let's create a church based on snake-handling. All of Jesus' disciples were men, so no women clergy. All of those are examples of proof texting.

The wiser approach is to check one verse or story against the whole of our knowledge. In this case of "God's dog," remember how Jesus treated everybody else. Remember your

---

[21] Rowe, David Johnson. *"God's Dog."* In *Fieldstones of Faith, Vol. II.* Lulu Press, 2011

own feelings about Jesus. Yes, feelings count. We do this all the time for friends, for people we respect. If we hear something about a friend that seems clearly out of character for them, we will delve deeper, look further, and put it in the context of the whole person. All scripture is profitable; some is just harder to get at.

Other scriptures lie in wait for us, ready when we are at just the right time. Many churches begin worship with Psalm 118:24, "This is the day the Lord has made! Let us rejoice and be glad in it." It is the perfect opening, a good "Stop/Look/Listen" way to start Church. It is a theological "good morning."

One summer I had a wedding in torrential rain, scheduled for outdoors on a picturesque lawn overlooking the Block Island harbor. Instead, the rains came hard.

Every wedding begins months, even years before, in the imagination of bride and groom, and parents. They picture it, plan it, pray for it. My Block Island wedding looked like a dream, at least during the rehearsal the night before. On Saturday it looked like a nightmare.

But it wasn't.

Inspired by the contagious, joyful spirit of the wedding couple, Alida and I stepped forward under the storm tent and began the wedding loud and clear.

This is the day the Lord has made.
Really, this is the day.
Let us rejoice and be glad!

And you know what? We did. At that rain-soaked wedding it was a perfect day, their day, this specific day given to them to celebrate love, and scripture helped make it so. The innate authority of scripture announcing it was a God-given, great day took on a power of its own. Believe me, through the years

I've tried all sorts of other rain-soaked openings, relying on my own wittiness, or hokey proverbs about rain being good luck, or just ignoring the obvious disappointment in the air, all met by pained smiles. However, hitting rain head-on with scripture made the day beautiful. It worked. The Bible is so much like most of life, the more work you put into it the more you get out of it. Therefore, work it.

The Bible is up to the challenge of being looked at critically; it invites us, "Come, let us reason together" (Isaiah 1:18). The art of preaching is the art of reasoning together, otherwise there is no need for preaching. When I am working on a sermon I pick some scripture, let it ramble around my head for a while, days, weeks, months. When I preach it the congregation takes it in and lets it ramble around their heads for a while. My reason mixes with their reason, all working through God's reason. The end result is profitable.

That interaction between people and scripture working together is wonderfully illustrated by a story in Acts 8 about Jesus' disciple, Philip, and his encounter with an Ethiopian government official. The man had been in Jerusalem to worship and was returning to Ethiopia where he was the Queen's treasurer. Philip was inspired by an angel to find the Ethiopian, who was sitting in his chariot, studying the Bible:

> *So Philip ran up to it and heard him reading the prophet Isaiah. He asked, "Do you understand what you are reading?" He replied, "How can I, unless someone guides me?" And he invited Philip to get in and sit beside him.* (Acts 8: 26-38)

The Ethiopian had been reading some of the famous verses from Isaiah about the promised Messiah, giving Philip the opportunity to make the connection between the man, the scripture, and the events that had just unfolded in Jerusalem

— Jesus' Holy Week of death and resurrection. Philip took the Ethiopian's spiritual seeking, linked it up with their shared ancient scriptures and his own contemporary experience, leading to an honest to goodness conversion. The story ends with the Ethiopian asking to be baptized right then and there.

What is instructive is that the Ethiopian's solitary pursuit of understanding is fulfilled by the introduction of a new person with fresh insights. That is the power of group Bible study, or Sunday worship, or seeing scripture through the eyes of an artist, a writer, a musician. The next time you are in a major museum, look for their collection of old European art. Gathered together in one area, usually, will be ten or twenty paintings depicting a scene from the life of Jesus. Nativities and crucifixions are the most popular, of course, but keep looking. You'll find Jesus conversing, inviting, teaching, healing, walking. There may be a painting of Jesus standing before Pilate, being judged, or lying lifeless at the foot of the cross after being taken down. Look at all of the paintings carefully, see the artist working with the scripture, taking all he had read or heard and forging his own understanding. One of my favorites is a two-sided painting by Giovanni Battista Cremonini (1595) at the Clark Museum. On one side is the Crucifixion; on the other, Jesus in the Garden of Gethsemane. In the Garden of Gethsemane painting, Jesus' whole body is arching upward, beseeching God, as the Bible confesses he did, "if it be possible, remove this cup from me" — his poignant plea to escape the cross (Matthew 26:39). Heaven's answer is stunningly, provocatively stark. Three little angels, three cherubs so popular in old Christian art, hover just above Jesus, holding out to him his cross, the nails, and the crown of thorns.

These artists are doing visually what the Bible does verbally, and what we do spiritually. We see Jesus as heroic, beatific, idealized, brutalized, pensive, confident, sorrowful, purposeful, peaceful, very human, very divine.

That is Bible Study, whether it is art or a group discussion or a powerful requiem or a simple sermon. When you feel the humanity of Jesus in that paradoxical partnership with his divinity, striving to be what you need God to be, then you understand what the Ethiopian was looking for, what compelled Philip to go find him, and the joy they experienced as they come together.

Jesus is central to understanding Scripture. I have spent my entire life connected with Church, and my whole career as a pastor. I was brought up with the Bible, converted by the Bible, studied it inside and out, taught it forever, and love it. I haven't avoided any scripture, text, or doctrine. I've tried to figure out the intricacies of Leviticus and the coded mysteries of Revelation. I have endured all the trends that have beset Christianity in my lifetime: fundamentalism, Pentecostalism, TV evangelism, liberalism, demythologizing, atheism, secularism, post-Christianity, doomsday prophets and God is Dead. With all the trends have come all the arguments over scriptures, doctrines built on scripture, social policies dictated by scriptures. Churches and denominations have fought over speaking in tongues, homosexuality, creationism, social justice, women's ordination, with Biblical verses as their weapon of choice.

I choose Jesus. Maybe I'm slow, or simple, or lazy, but after trying a long time to fully grasp the whole Bible I had to admit that I could not take it all in, I couldn't master it all or make it all a priority.

Instead, I choose Jesus. To put it bluntly, as the rest of the Bible fits in with Jesus, that's great. Where it doesn't, I don't worry about it. We all pick our allegiances, our priorities. I pick Jesus, and the scriptures found in Matthew, Mark, Luke and John that give us his essence.

From time to time I do a program for our high school youth group. First, I open with two powerful scriptures with the same point. Joshua demands that the people of Israel make a choice, "Choose this day whom thou shalt serve" (Joshua 24:15). Five hundred years later Elijah throws down the same challenge, "How long halt ye between two opinions?" (1 Kings 18:21).

Then I present three scenarios drawn from current news or daily life, each with three options for their behavior. As they choose an option they go to a different corner of the room, explain their choices to one another and then to the group. There is no sitting on the sidelines. Then we bring the discussion back to the center: Jesus. Yes, it's a cliché, but what would Jesus do? In our ministry that is our choice.

Choosing Jesus is not the easy way out. Try reading Jesus' Sermon on the Mount, just three chapters in Matthew (5-7). In short order he totally redefines happiness in the Beatitudes, telling us to embrace the blessedness of mourning, meekness, peacemaking and persecution. At that, he is only getting warmed up. He takes some scripture and deepens it, telling us that killing and adultery are not the real problem, we need to stop our lust and anger. Get to the core. Plus, stop judging, stop worrying; start forgiving, start turning the other cheek and going the extra mile. While you're at it, love your enemies, don't resist evil, no more "eye for an eye" even if it says so in the Bible. Be perfect, and do unto others as you would like to be done unto. That is not the easy way out.

My greatest challenge is to live my life figuring out how to live those three chapters. This leaves no time for the six or seven Bible verses against homosexuality, or deciphering the exact date of Jesus' Second Coming based on Daniel and Revelation, or determining who gets into heaven and who doesn't (hint: it has to do with love), or explaining predestination.

One autumn I took our youth group on a retreat in New Hampshire. Eventually they wanted a break from all my programming. They wanted to play Frisbee. We drove to a nearby Christian summer camp, and asked permission to use their playing field. The Director was quite pleased to see a church group of teenagers, immediately agreed, reached into his desk and presented me with a list of at least twenty doctrines I had to affirm in order for my Christian youth to use his Christian camp to play Frisbee. I couldn't even understand half of them. The camp was either pre-Millenialist or post-Millenialist, who can figure that out? They were anti-charismatic and pro-inerrancy and against baptizing infants.

We just wanted to play Frisbee. So, yes, I signed, but all I really wanted to say was, "Jesus," not as an epithet but as a summary, i.e. "We believe in Jesus." Period.

Somewhat tongue in cheek, I have come up with a document I use, loftily titled, "The Absolute Essentials of the Christian Faith." It came from the idea that if I were to meet a stranger who claims to be Christian there ought to be a few things I could assume about them. And that could be assumed about me.

My life has been full of Christians whose behavior and statements surprised me. I have been fired, betrayed, robbed, beaten, propositioned, stabbed in the back, blackballed, lied to and lied about, all by people proudly professing their Christianity. In Kinshasa, a soldier at a checkpoint put a machine gun in my face, and robbed me – and then was thrilled to discover I was a Christian. "I'm a Christian, too," my new friend exulted.

So, in frustration, I put down on paper my assumptions about being a Christian. Not surprisingly, most of them pointed back to Love, beginning with John 3:16: "For God so loved the world that he gave his only begotten son, that whosoever believeth in him shall not perish, but have everlasting life."

Whoever first said it is right: that is indeed "the Gospel in a nutshell." Everything else emanates from that. Jesus, the Church, mission, evangelism, when done right and understood right it all comes from that driver, "God so loved the world."

Once we grasp that, then the Old Testament prophets' stern demand for justice and righteousness, Jesus' Great Commission to "go ye into all the world" (Matthew 28:19) and Paul's soaring "faith, hope and love abide, but the greatest of these is love" (1 Corinthians 13:13), all make sense. The Lord's Prayer, The Beatitudes, the Parables, the Cross all make sense. Even the troubling and puzzling stories can be seen in a new light. Love can do that.

In writing the biography of my Indian dear friend, Azariah, I asked him for his favorite Bible verse. "Oh, all the verses about love," was his answer. That led me to John's epistles which echo Jesus' life and teachings, and provide a perfect circle of love, a complete rationale for God at work in the universe. It starts with a delightful verse, "How great is the love which God has lavished upon us" (1 John 3:1). "Lavish" is an old fashioned word, like abundance, *abbondanza,* an over-the-top love, much like a grandparents' love, so much it is almost embarrassing.

But how do we know that? John answers, "this is how we know what love is: Jesus laid down his life for us" (1 John 3:16). What a perfect mirror to Jesus' own definitional statement, "there is no greater love than this, that you lay down your life for your friends" (John 15:13). Okay, but why would God do this? Well, "God is love" (1 John 4:16). That gets to the heart of the matter, doesn't it? The Bible has tried to tell us as much since Genesis but, as Paul says, we don't always see clearly until finally this profound truth is laid out in lavender so we can't miss it (1 Corinthians 13:9-13). God is love; that is God's nature, God's essence, God can't do anything else but love. Whatever is loving is Godly. Whatever is not loving is, well, not Godly, or is ungodly, or anti-Godly.

All right, if we have all this love lavished upon us, what is our response? Whenever we receive something nice we want to respond in kind, return the favor, be nice back, at least say "thanks." What is our Bible-based response to such "amazing grace" love?

John completes the circle just as we would want to complete the circle, but with a surprising twist. God turns our love outward. "This is how we know we love ... by loving God and carrying out God's commands ... whoever loves God must also love ... since God so loved us, we ought to love one another" (1 John 4: 7-21). With that little reminder to "carry out God's commands," we circle back to Jesus' exacting and specific commands on this very topic: "Love your neighbor ... Love your enemies ... Love one another" (Matthew 19:19; Matthew 5:44; John 13:35). That about covers it. We are at the heart of God by looking at the heart of Jesus, which is at the heart of the Bible.

A chapter on my love affair with the Bible has turned into a chapter on my love affair with Jesus. Maybe that is as it should be, for me. I am intrigued by preachers I hear on TV who claim to have discovered the Bible's secrets to wealth, or the role of the Soviet Union/UN/Iran in knowing the date of Christ's return, or to explaining the Trinity. Sorry, I don't get any of that.

I am stuck with Jesus, and whether it is Jesus who unlocks the door to the Bible or the other way around, take your pick, I do not have the savvy for that, either.

By choice, I am left with Jesus. Certainly my theology, as with the rest of me, is the product of my environment, my life experiences. The hymns declare:

I've found a friend, oh such a friend ...

He walks with me and talks with me ...

Day by day, three things I pray:
to see Thee more clearly,
to love Thee more dearly,
to follow Thee more nearly,
day by day.[22]

Amen to that. Way, way back when, when I was running my Coffee House ministry, we showed a documentary about Leonard Cohen. Cohen, legendary folksinger, a Jewish/Buddhist Canadian, stated, "I've always had an awful fascination with Jesus." It took me a while to make Jesus my fascination. Once I did, other aspects of life and ministry fell into place ... including scripture. Thank you, Jesus.

---

[22] Small, James G. *I've Found a Friend.* The Revival Hymn Book, second series, 1863. Miles, C. Austin. *In the Garden.* 1912. Schwartz, Stephen. *Day by Day.* Written for the musical "Godspell." 1971.

SEVEN

My Journey from Preacher to Pastor: Monkey Hands and Elephant Ears

I learned to preach in an empty church. I learned to pray when my boss pulled a sneaky trick on me. I learned pastoral care from a man who couldn't do anything.

Preaching, praying, and pastoral care, the three essential "P's" of being a pastor. In short, I started out to be a preacher, ended up being a pastor, and learned to pray along the way.

The First P: Preaching

After it became clear that I was not going to be a Major League baseball player and save the Chicago Cubs from oblivion, and after I was personally saved from oblivion, I set out to become a preacher. Midway through seminary I was fired from a church for anti-Vietnam war activity. Among the insults hurled at me by the Pastor was this assessment, "You don't have a prayer of being a preacher."

Preaching is vitally important to Church. Historically it is the centerpiece of Protestant Christianity. In Catholicism the altar is at the heart of worship, the Priest performs the mystery of the Mass, dramatically transforming wine and wafer into the literal blood and body of Jesus. Christ is the host at his own sacrificial feast, and the worshipper, led by the Priest, is invited to partake.

In much of Protestantism the pulpit is the most prominent place in the sanctuary, front and center, often raised up high above the congregation. One Sunday I was a guest preacher at an old, historic church. As I climbed the winding stairs up to the pulpit, when my eyes got level to the

111

pulpit there was a simple but powerful sign: "We would see Jesus" (John 12:21). It was a reminder that people weren't there to see me. Preachers come and go, clergy come and go. What causes churches to endure is that we have an enduring message, a message centered on the life and teachings of Jesus. In one form or another people come to church to "see Jesus." Preaching is the Protestant most way to help people "see Jesus."

That is intimidating, as is St. Paul's explanation of why preaching is so important:

Paul
epistle
to
Romans

> *How, then, can someone call on the one they have not believed in? And how can they believe in the one of whom they have not heard? And how can they hear without someone preaching to them? And how can they preach unless they are sent? As it is written, "how beautiful are the feet of those who bring good news!"*
>
> *(Romans 10: 14-15)*

If I had known that verse when I was nineteen I might not have been in such a rush to become a preacher. Paul makes it sound daunting, urgent, vital, as if the whole soul of someone depended on my preaching. But I was much more like a child ready to play "dress up," pretending to be some grown up role model of a preacher without grasping the real role.

Wanting to be a preacher and becoming one were two different things. It intrigues me that I self-identified so early as a preacher rather than as a pastor, minister, Reverend, or clergy. My father was an extraordinary role model across the whole spectrum of ministry. Indeed, it was his "man for all seasons," "Jack of all trades" approach to church work that appealed so much to me. Above all, he was a craftsman in the pulpit in the classic, Post World War II, 1950s mode that made the word "pulpiteer" high praise. Dad was a pulpiteer.

Working on his sermon, crafting it as surely as any artisan, pulling together perfect illustrations from the classics to highlight his scripture for each sermon, this consumed much of his week. He never had an "office," it was always his "study." He never excused himself to write a sermon, he would go "off to study." Preaching is a work of art, and it is as much work as art. My father would estimate, as I do, that he spent twenty hours working on a sermon. (rhetoric, applied!)

Interestingly, when he retired at 86 after almost seventy years in ministry, I asked him why he retired. He answered, "It stopped being fun to prepare a sermon." He still had the energy, the health, the ability, he still did all the work well, his church still wanted him. But when the joy goes out of preaching, the study, the preparation, the crafting, then, as an old athlete would say, "it's time to hang 'em up."

preaching needs to be fueled by joy

I could have asked him, as people always ask me, "Don't you have a backlog of old sermons? Can't you just pick one out, dust it off, preach it again? Nobody will know." It is meant as kind advice for an overworked or tired or rushed preacher. But some of us from the "old school" would see that as insulting to preachers and to hearers.

On a practical level, it is harder to rework an old sermon for a new day than to start fresh. I've done it, and it doesn't work. On a spiritual level, preaching is a three way partnership between God, the preacher and the congregation. We all come to church having lived out the experiences of the week before. My own particular emphasis all week has been to try to figure out what God wants us to work through for that Sunday. My preparation begins early in the week and continues until a few minutes before church. During that whole time I am in constant communication with God, including this rather simple, stock prayer: "God, help me to understand what you need me to say, and what my people need to hear. Prepare the hearts and minds and spirits of our church family to hear my sermon. Where I am right, make it clear. Where I'm wrong, distract them so they don't hear it, or help them to forget it. God, go before my sermon, be within it, follow after."

That's the David Rowe version of the more popular pre-sermon proclamation, "May the words of my mouth, and the meditation of all our hearts, be acceptable in thy sight, our Rock and our Redeemer" (Psalm 19:14). Both recognize that good preaching, successful preaching, is teamwork. When you and I and God bring our full selves into the sermon, magic happens. When any one of the three is missing, it's a dud.

So, no recycled sermons.

My training in preaching began with seminary. No one entered seminary with less training than I. What little I did know I did not yet know that I knew. As time went on, year by year, I began to factor in what I had learned growing up, watching my father in action, going to Sunday School, absorbing all kinds of sermons right through college. Little by little, all those lessons kicked in, what I wanted to do and not do, what I liked or didn't like, what worked and what didn't.

Late in the afternoon of my first day at Andover Newton Seminary I called my father and told him I was quitting. The day had been filled with placement exams, testing what we knew about the world of religion and Church. The test included words and ideas I had never heard: hermeneutics, homiletics, redaction criticism, eschatology, theology. In college I majored in Anthropology-Sociology, and never took a course in religion.

I was out of my element and it was only the first day. Wisely, my father told me to talk with the Dean. The Dean, perhaps exaggerating, said that I was the best kind of first year student. I knew nothing, and I knew that I knew nothing. I didn't come in with preconceptions and stuff that needed to be unlearned. He called me an "empty canvas" that they could now fill. Then he told me about Jeremiah, some Old Testament prophet I had never read. In the Book of Jeremiah, chapter 8, the prophet is told by God to visit a potter's shed, to watch the potter take clay, mold it, shape it and reshape it until it was good for something. That, the Dean told me, was what they were going to do with me. I was their clay.

Or silly putty.

The first few weeks continued to offer proof that I had no idea what was going on. One day featured an ecclesiastical job fair. Andover Newton is conveniently located in Newton Center, a lovely suburb just outside of Boston. Within an hour's radius were hundreds of churches and social service agencies willing to hire young seminarians.

In those days seminary enrollment was almost entirely young and male. It would be another decade or more before the seminary world changed dramatically in two ways. First, by the arrival of women. Women had always experienced the call to pastoral ministry, but had been discouraged or even prevented from answering it. In the 1970's, women began entering seminaries and challenging the hiring practices of churches and denominations. And secondly, people in midlife began to show up in seminaries, men and women choosing to change their lives mid-career. Many had felt called when they were younger, but it took life's twists and turns to get them to say "yes." A decade after my Andover-Newton years, these changes began happening.

But most of the students of my era were as they had always been. Young men, fresh from college, full of idealism, entered seminary prepared to save the world and the Church. The Vietnam War was raging, the Civil Rights Movement continued to stir the national conscience, American society and its churches were torn apart by deep divisions. I distinctly remember not only late night bull sessions but also classroom discussions when we would boldly proclaim that once we graduated and were ordained everything would be better. Just wait.

That job fair during my first weeks was an eye opener. Churches were looking for youth pastors, with more emphasis on youth and little on pastor. I took a job at a nearby Congregational church, helping to lead junior high and senior high youth groups, teaching Sunday School. The city of Newton paid me to run a drop-in center after school in the church basement, and we parlayed that into a weekly Coffee House. I can't emphasize enough how great these experiences were. Throughout seminary I was immersed in every kind of youth ministry, and loved every minute of it.

Nevertheless, by the winter of our last year a few of us realized that we were woefully unprepared to become church leaders, real pastors and preachers. We petitioned Andover Newton to allow us to create a multi-disciplinary course on the practical, day-to-day side of church life. Given the times, I could do draft counseling, track down runaways, deal with drugs and abortion, work Jethro Tull and the Who into any youth meeting, convince a generation of teenagers that Church was "relevant," which was the coin of the age. But budgets, funerals, board meetings, visitations, weddings, preaching ... adult stuff? I was not ready.

Maybe bull sessions were a training ground for preaching, I don't know. Good ones were full of ideas and words hoping to persuade, inspire, change. But the best training ground for preaching was preaching. In one preaching course we had to prepare a sermon, videotape it before our classmates, and then watch it together. Fortunately, I did not need any critique. I was so awful that no one needed to point out anything. There I was, sprawled over the pulpit, my Sixties long hair falling over my face, offering a caricature of nonchalance. I was so eager to be hip and relevant, counting on my mumbling to seem as earnest as Bob Dylan. Instead, I came across as simply not caring. I did not care enough to stand up, to speak clearly, or to offer a cogent thought. My carefully constructed indifference looked like I was indifferent toward the scripture, the sermon and the congregation. It was either time to revive my baseball career or to grow up.

Quickly, I started buying books of sermons, hunting through used book stores. Once upon a time sermon collections were big business in the publishing world, so I found plenty and started to preach them. For years, at whatever church I was serving, I would go into the sanctuary at night, long after everyone was gone, so I could have it to myself. With my stack of sermon books I'd go to the pulpit, open up to random sermons and start preaching. I preached great old American revivalists like D.L. Moody and Sam Jones, and popular 20th century legends like Billy Graham, Norman Vincent Peale, and Harry Emerson Fosdick.

I tried to imagine and imitate their gestures, intonations, emphases, then make them my own. Was it Demosthenes who taught his students elocution, public speaking, by having them practice speeches after filling their mouths with pebbles? That is how it felt as I attempted the archaic sentence structure and word selection and thinking processes of great preachers from other centuries and places.

The times may have changed but the challenge was and is the same as ever. Whether it is Jesus on a hillside preaching his Sermon on the Mount or Peter at Pentecost or Paul in Athens, every preacher believes they have something important to say or they wouldn't be trying to say it. However, the preacher's audience is always made up of people whose lives are full of every disarray and distraction imaginable. On any given Sunday someone in the congregation has lost their job, or gotten bad news, or is holding a squirming child, or planning a wedding, or fighting a cold, or just moved, or is preparing for surgery, or is in sorrow, or got a promotion, or just retired, or is worried, fearful, overjoyed, struggling, needy or hopeful.

Yet they have managed to make it to church, and the first half hour is easy enough. A four minute hymn, a two minute scripture, a three minute prayer, a five minute musical piece, things are kept moving, you even stand up and sit down a couple of times. Then comes the sermon, which cannot end until the preacher stops. Until then the congregation is a captive audience. The preacher's task is to break through that whole spectrum of human concern and distraction, and bring forth an understanding of scripture that makes sense for that person in that pew that day.

The delightful reward of preaching is when the right sermon on the right day for the right person all comes together. It happens often enough to make preaching worth the effort.

One of my seminary professors told us, "When you preach a sermon, especially a really good one, one where you know for sure it really connected, when you get home tear it up and burn it. God meant it for that day."

Another professor gave equally vital advice: "When you're angry at someone about something, and you want to preach a sermon against it, go ahead. Sit down, write that sermon, get all your righteous anger down on paper. Then preach it loud right there in your office. And then tear it up, and go write what God wants you to write."

Both professors knew that worship opens the door for magic to take place. Somebody is sitting there in Church who needs your preaching, so you'd better be prepared, or, as my father would put it, you'd better "study." Study means to put the work in to connect that scripture to that person without even knowing who that person is. That is the delightful mystery of preaching.

Jesus at least had the luxury of creating scripture. The rest of us have to find scripture for our jumping off point. Sooner or later in every sermon we have to grapple with the scripture, and see where life leads us while tethered to that scripture.

One of the great joys of preaching is the moment when people greet you after worship and say, "David, you were preaching right at me! How did you know what I needed? How did you know my situation?" Of course, I didn't. But God did. That's why I had crossed out a paragraph, added a story, picked a specific scripture, took it in a certain direction, worked and reworked it, crossed out even more in order to highlight a key moment.

Crossing out may be as important to a sermon as writing. I joke with my father that the best thing he taught me was how to use a black magic marker. Whenever I visited he would have me guest preach for him and Saturday night was always the time for the black magic marker as he crossed out words and sentences, whole paragraphs and pages, arguing with me every step of the way about how to get to the meat of it.

One summer I attended Sunday worship at the Advent Christian Camp Meeting in Mechanic Falls, Maine. "Camp meeting" was and is an old fashioned summertime worship life among Christians in some parts of America. Families would come together, stay in little cottages or tents or whatever the precursor was to an RV, and spend a week or two of worship, study, and fun. My grandfather led this campground, my father grew up there, and I visited several times.

The preacher was working hard that Sunday, exhorting us all to be expectant and ready for Christ's triumphant return to earth, his "Second Coming." Building to a crescendo, his false teeth popped out in midsentence. He grabbed his teeth in midair, put them back in, declared, "That always happens when I bite into the Word of God," and kept on preaching.

Whether in a humorous setting or not, the Word of God is a serious and weighty matter, worthy of being capitalized. In any Church that values worship and preaching, liberal or conservative, it is always essential to "bite into the Word of God." Even that image infers that the Bible is, like food, something to be prepared, dissected, chewed over, digested, and turned into energy. The same for a sermon since, at best, sermon and scripture serve each other. And each, ultimately, has the same purpose. Scripture and sermon both exist to bring the reader or listener closer to God.

One winter I attended a conference at my old seminary near Boston when we were hit with a huge snowstorm. The keynote preacher was Dr. Gardner Taylor, one of the giants of American preaching. The school had invited a Gospel Choir from Boston to sing. It is not an exaggeration to say that, aside from Dr. Taylor and the Choir, there were a dozen people. I fully expected the service to be cancelled or abbreviated, but instead the man preached like his life depended on it. Or mine.

That was precisely the point for Dr. Taylor. Later on he and I had the chance to talk and reflect on that evening. For him it was very clear. That sermon might well be the last of his life, God could have called him home that night or the next day. Or for someone in the congregation that could have been their last night on earth, their last sermon to hear, their last chance to connect with God. Either way, Taylor was motivated to preach his heart out; preaching matters that much.

Yes, preaching to a dozen is as important as preaching to a crowd. But it is also true that preachers love an audience. So it was a great Sunday for me when a new family – three generations' worth – decided to begin worshiping at my church. They filled two entire pews, listening attentively to my sermons. This went on for three months. And then they quit the church.

"You don't preach the blood," the family matriarch explained, "I need my family to hear about the blood, every week." She was referring to the blood of Jesus, specifically the blood that poured from Jesus' side and hands and feet and brow as he died on the cross for our sins. Echoing the concerns of St. Paul, that grandmother was only wondering, "How can my dear family believe if they don't hear? And how will they hear if someone doesn't preach?" To me, furthermore, she was crying, "You're not preaching." At least, not what mattered to her.

We can quibble over theology, but Taylor and the grandmother were both telling me that preaching matters. I am not saying that I now "preach the blood" every Sunday. But every Sunday I am completely aware that in my sermon I want folks to see Jesus. I know that someone in the pew needs what God has troubled me enough to say, and that my sermon, however humble, matters.

The Second P: Prayer

Prayer isn't preaching. That may be the first lesson of praying. It can be hard for a preacher to turn off the preaching, the result being that every pronouncement or conversation sounds like a sermon. At family dinners or at church meetings the pastor can too easily resort to preaching rather than listening, sharing, or having a conversation.

Prayer is conversation with God, that is the beginning and end of it. Even public prayer is just public conversation with God. It is not a time to send a message to the congregation, that's what the sermon is for. Nor is it time to talk to God as if

121

God is out of the loop or unaware of world events. It is time, privately or publicly, to share what is on your heart.

I learned to pray the hard way. By the time I was ordained I had developed a praying style not much different from my preaching style. I would write it, agonize over it, building thoughts and points into strong statements, aiming for profundity and inspiration, using hooks like repetition or alliterations, various tricks of the trade.

After seminary I joined the staff of a large, thriving Baptist Church in Haverhill, Massachusetts. Our Sunday service was broadcast live on radio. As the junior minister, I never got to preach much, so the Pastoral Prayer was my chance to shine. I spent hours writing out my prayers ahead of time. One Sunday, just at the moment I was about to start reading my carefully crafted, word-smithed, highly polished prayer, the old pastor reached over, grabbed my papers, and whispered in my ear, "time to learn how to pray, boy."

Time to learn how to pray. Boy, was he ever right. The Bible says, "Pray without ceasing" (1 Thessalonians 5:17), suggesting that our relationship with God should be second nature to us, as normal as breathing, something with immediacy and intimacy. Forget holy language filled with Thee and Thou, forget using a particular sonorous voice that clergy often take on for public prayer. Just do it. Talk with God.

So, that's what I did that Sunday morning at the First Baptist Church of Haverhill, live on radio, when the boss stole my carefully written prayer. I learned to talk with God, spontaneously, from the heart, without worrying. We sing, "What a friend we have in Jesus, all our sins and griefs to bear, what a privilege to carry everything to God in prayer."

Well, then, just do it. It is liberating to normalize our own prayer life so that we speak easily and intimately out loud, or confidently and bluntly within ourselves. That takes some getting used to, offering words to God at any time and place, about anything. I've worked at it, I'm getting better, but it still takes effort. I need to remind myself that God really does like to hear from me, not just in moments of crisis.

I'm new to the generation of instant communication. Smartphones, Skype, Instagram, Facebook all make it possible to "communicate without ceasing." While this is natural for the younger half of the world, my mind doesn't work that way, not yet. I still telephone my daughter, who lives in India, when it's a special occasion or there's news to share: "Oh, I'm having knee surgery ... oh, happy birthday! .... oh, Merry Christmas." It took me a long time to realize that I can contact someone halfway around the world – someone I love! – just to check in, any old time. As a result, I missed a lot, but I'm getting better.

It is equally true of prayer. To pray without ceasing realizes a whole different relationship than, "Oh, I need a favor ... oh, I'm in trouble ... oh, help me, please." Little by little, on a personal level, I am learning to send a thought to God, opening up a conversation that always goes in surprising ways. Always.

On a pastoral level I have been quicker to pray at a moment's notice. Early on it was clear that I needed to have a ready prayer whenever invited to dinner. "With the Reverend here, why doesn't he say grace?" is a popular refrain. As I moved fully into the world of mission it was certain that I would always be asked to pray and preach. In India, after every service, people line up for individual prayer, a powerful testimony. I don't speak Telugu or Hindi, they don't speak English. I have no inkling of their prayer request, they have no idea what I am saying. Yet the expectation is that prayer hugely matters, that God understands even when we do not. All of this pushes me to be more ever ready to pray.

We carry this intentionally into our pastoral church life. There is a need for immediacy and intimacy throughout a church family. For too long in my career, conversations or phone calls would end either with a plea ("David, say a prayer for me") or with a promise from me ("I'll keep you in my prayers"). That would be the end of it. The matter we were discussing was important enough that the person had stepped out of their usual reticence or reserve to admit a need for God's help. Or I had sensed enough urgency to offer God's help. Then, as the moment passed, that prayer need would compete with a thousand other concerns for space in my mind and my time. Would I remember that prayer promise later that day, or the next Sunday during the pastoral prayer?

Gradually, I learned to deal with immediacy immediately. If somebody cries out for help, they probably mean now. I began to look for ways to pray right away. That was obvious and acceptable during hospital visits. A hospital visit, by definition, is a matter of urgency; no one is in the hospital for fun. It is always a time of worry, pain, fear, uncertainty, and a brush with mortality. Hospital visitation is a top priority, and I have visited thousands of people in every imaginable condition, spiritually as well as physically.

Only one person has refused my offer for personal prayer, right then and there, as we were holding hands. Sharing prayer has always felt natural, and right, and obvious. But one time, in the ICU, as I took a man's hand and said my usual, "Let's have a word of prayer," he startled me with a firm "no, thank you." I hope I didn't show my surprise as I wished him well. Several hours later he called me. The doctor had just been with him. Surgery was scheduled for the next day, and the outcome was iffy. Would I be willing to come back and pray with him?

I did, without saying anything about his change of mind. I understood. My own prayer life has too often been an up-and-down thing, up when I want something, down when life is good. This is most stark when I fly. I hate flying, I don't understand flight, and it scares the heck out of me. This makes me a multi-prayer flyer, including an obligatory visit to the airport chapel before boarding. Yet it has continually amazed me how rarely I remember to offer a gratitude prayer once safely landed. It is such a glaring omission, an embarrassing spiritual deficit, that I decided to confess it in Sunday sermons before every trip, counting on peer pressure and the knowledge that everyone would ask about it to motivate me. Evidently, gratitude wasn't enough motivation, but embarrassment is working, as I am now improving at making prayer second nature.

Prayer is a strange mix, even among those who believe in it. We want it, need it, offer or request it. Everyone has stories of its efficacy, however mysterious. Yet we are hesitant, embarrassed, forgetful about it. It is like praying to St. Anthony whenever I lose something. It works, I have no idea why; it should be embarrassing for me as a saint-less Protestant Congregationalist. But St. Anthony is undefeated in my personal lost and found history.

Prayer works. Yes, it's a cliché but true enough because of another cliché: prayer changes things. The very nature of articulating, putting into words your most personal thoughts and needs, starts a healthy process. Put that together with opening yourself up to a dimension outside yourself and you create an environment for change. Prayer works and prayer changes things. With prayer comes clarity, focus, even honesty. Without getting into theology or doctrine, if you believe in prayer you no doubt believe someone is listening, and that someone, that "higher power," is worthy of respect. You are not going to lie in prayer. You might lie to yourself, but it is silly and counterproductive to lie to God. You wouldn't go to an orthopedic surgeon for knee pain and declare that your knee was fine. Something propelled you to that doctor visit, you are with the someone you believe can help, so you 'fess up. You tell what hurts, how it happened, what you've tried, how it failed, express your hopes, and ask for help.

Prayer offers the same opportunity for honesty. One of the most valuable lessons I ever learned about prayer came from a pastor I've long since forgotten, but he taught the idea of a "Prayer Covenant." A pastor is often presented with one side of a story and expected to offer advice, prayer support and personal encouragement without access to the full story. In a Prayer Covenant, two people – in this case, I and the person speaking with me— make an agreement to pray about the specific matter and the facts presented every day, for thirty days, at exactly the same time. You don't have to be together, but you agree to be in prayer at the same time. You are linked together and with God, spiritually, wherever you are.

The power of the idea rests on key assumptions. One, thirty days is a long time; it takes commitment. Two, nobody is going to lie to God for thirty days. Either they will stop praying, or start being honest. Day by day, prayer by prayer, the dynamic changes, perspective changes, facts change. With all that change there is room for God to work.

A person came to me to explain why he was divorcing his wife, putting all the blame on her countless faults and failures. He would not allow me to talk with her but did agree to do the thirty day prayer covenant, praying about his marriage and divorce every morning at 7:00. To his credit he took it seriously; he was someone who believed that God was listening. Therefore, he was one of those people who would either stop praying or get real. He chose to get real. Each week he checked in with me, accepting more of the blame until, in the fourth week, he took major responsibility for their problems, and they reconciled. Prayer works. Prayer changes things.

Modern technology has greatly helped pastoral prayer to be immediate. During one Lenten season, Alida and I hosted a luncheon in New York City for church members who worked in the city. That same morning there had been a tragic commuter train crash in another part of the country, and it was heavy on people's hearts, especially these New York commuters. "Wouldn't it have been wonderful," a businessperson suggested, "if you had sent out a prayer for commuters to all of us right after that happened." Not long after, the Columbine school massacre took place, and we sent out our first "email blast" prayer. For our people we were with them, linked together with God in a mystical, immediate, personal way. 9/11, the Newtown school massacre, the Charleston killings, the Iraq and Afghanistan Wars, San Bernardino, and the Paris massacre and other concerns that cry out for "the beloved community" have all unleashed the power of prayer to jump space and bring us together, thanks to the immediacy of technology.

As more communication comes to us instantaneously, the need and opportunity to respond instantly is very real. I used to think that emails were like fine wine or good cheese, better left alone to age. Slowly I have learned not only to hit "read" but also "reply." The opportunities to reply with a spur of the moment, very specific, truly intimate prayer are, to my Luddite mind, a miracle. Yet there they are, hour by hour.

A typical email could be, "David, I'm in the ER with Mom, think she had a stroke." Or, "Hi, hate to trouble you, know you're busy. Family problems. Pray for us." Once I learned to actually reply to email, my notes were full of pious platitudes, varieties of "hang in there," and "you'll be in my prayers." Eventually, like Newton being hit by the gravitational pull of an apple, it dawned on me. Why simply promise future prayers? Why not pray? Right then and there, at the computer keyboard, in my reply email ... even with my e.e.cummings style of no capitals and lousy punctuation, why not pray with them immediately? So I started. "Here is a prayer for right now," I reply, and then type a prayer for that person with that concern, as specific and personal as it would be if I were with them, holding hands.

Frankly, the response has been overwhelming, and telling. I learned pastoring in an age when visitation was central to ministry, literally a physical presence, one on one, face to face, bed side, hospital room, nursing home, living room, office, court room, prison cell, bar stool, restaurant, eye to eye. I understood that world, but today's world requires a different *modus operandi*, way of doing. Privacy laws, security concerns, the decline of religious influence, changes in medical practice often make it necessary to be in touch from a distance. Prayer bridges that distance. So while I can miss the old ways, I am starting to grab hold of the new ways.

Can this get awkward? Ask my son, Aaron. On the day we moved him into college, after all the boxes had been hauled into his dorm room, it was time for his emotional parents to say goodbye. But not just yet. First, I invited Aaron and the roommate he had just met to hold hands with us as I prayed over them. It seemed like a good idea at the time, and maybe it was, but yes, it was awkward. The same awkwardness pops up at restaurants and meetings. Do you pray out loud at McDonald's, or bow your head before a working lunch with coworkers? Awkward or not, people appreciate prayer in person ... or by email.

If this was a book about prayer I would get further into how to pray, when and what to pray. I would deal with the ever-present disappointment of prayers that don't go our way. Instead, I am focused on Church, and with the role that prayer plays in church life. My bottom line is that prayer is a mystery, it works, I don't understand it all, and it is a huge part of church life, all wrapped up in the mystery that is faith. I'm still learning how to do it, and getting more comfortable with doing it always, about anything.

The same pastor who yanked away my written prayer used to drive us into Boston for meetings. In the church parking lot, before he started the car, he would pray that God would open up a parking space for us on Tremont Street, one of the busiest streets in Boston. I thought it was stupid. Every single time there was a parking meter just for us. I still thought it was stupid.

The older I get the more comfortable I am with being stupid. In Jesus' first miracle, he turns water into wine so that a young couple's wedding reception won't be cut short (John 2:1-11). In the grand scheme of things, in my small mind, it was sort of a stupid miracle. Alida has taught me to embrace that miracle with the thought that what's important to us is important to God. For that couple in ancient Cana, their wedding reception was the most important thing in their lives. Jesus understood. If it's on your mind it's on God's mind. That opens up a whole world of immediacy and intimacy waiting for God's touch. Church, and church prayer, is a vehicle to make it happen.

The Third P: Pastoral Care

He wanted to die. So he stopped eating. And he probably saved my career.

I went into ministry, fresh from my own conversion, to save the Church and change the world. Around me was a world in turmoil at every turn. The Civil Rights era was reaching its peak, the anti-Vietnam movement was full-bore, the "Summer of Love" was anything but as drugs began to take their toll. An excellent book about 1965, *Eve of Destruction*, was both the title of a song and the feel of the age. Vietnam was a meat-grinder, cities were a burning cauldron, campuses majored in protest. Our various heroes were assassinated, and even God was dead, we were told.

It was just as God was declared dead that I decided to be a preacher. The arrogance of youth and the passion of a new convert convinced many of my generation that we were the Savior the Church needed. Listen to us, follow us as we tear apart your tired traditions, your rigid doctrines, and your fossilized institutions – that was our message. For me, at least, that messianic posturing lasted into the 70s. By the time I got involved with Habitat for Humanity we boasted that we were "A New Frontier in Christian Mission," rectifying two centuries of mission done poorly. We were not subtle.

Perhaps every generation sees itself that way, the just in timely corrective to all that has gone wrong before. I don't even want to think about how I must have sounded and appeared to all those folks who had labored so lovingly to keep those churches open that would one day employ a shaggy-haired, self-absorbed, strident know it all. Me.

I didn't know it at the time but the one thing that kept me palatable and employable was my commitment to pastoral care. Whether by instinct or the example of my father I knew that nothing was more important than taking care of business, and the business of a pastor is to care for the people. Pastoral Care. All the Jesus talk about the Good Shepherd really knowing his sheep, the sheep knowing his voice, and the wolves kept at bay turned out to be true (John 10: 1-18). Pastor, pastoral, pasture, sheep, shepherd, flock, all that terminology and imaging is fairly accurate for church life.

I asked my father when he finally knew he was a good pastor. He said it was around age forty, when he knew he was no longer going to change the world or save Christianity, and focused on caring for people. Pastoral Care. People care.

The man who wanted to die, stopped eating and saved my career was a patient at a state hospital. My seminary required its students to do "Clinical Pastoral Education," CPE, a euphemism for hell, or so we felt. It was an arduous experience on every level. We would-be pastors started off as orderlies, emptying bed pans, gofers for everybody. Whatever hierarchy existed in the hospital we were at the bottom. Once sufficiently humiliated we became junior chaplains, assigned specific patients who were subjected to our incompetence, inexperience, insensitivity. I had plenty of all three.

Among my patients on one ward were four men who could do nothing. Nothing. Whatever you imagine "nothing" to be, that was the full range of what they could do. My job was to roll them side to side from time to time, feed them by dropping spoonfuls of food into their mouths the way I had seen mother birds do for baby birds. For variety I changed TV channels, and carried on one way conversations met with blank stares or wild gesticulations. This one fellow wore a Boston Red Sox cap, so I would put a Red Sox game on the radio or television.

CPE was a brutal experience emotionally, spiritually, physically. The constant onslaught of need and human misery had the absurd result of making me feel sorry for myself. Self-pity in a sea of misery is not an attractive trait, but my story gets worse.

By Fridays I was yearning to get out, get home, get anywhere but there. On one particular Friday I had a chance to leave the hospital early, as soon as I had fed my four non-communicative men. Feeding was a slow process, and that day I rushed it. The Red Sox fan always drank slowly from a cup nestled under his armpit, through a long straw. I couldn't wait for that, so I opened his mouth, poured his drink in, went home, and had a nice weekend.

Next week, doing my rounds, I was told that my Red Sox fan had refused to eat or drink since Friday. He refused to wear his Red Sox hat, refused eye contact. He was shriveling up. Turns out my man *could* do something. He was not the nothing that I had determined him to be. In all the years of his life he had mastered something: he had learned to drink through a straw. And his one independent, proud accomplishment I had stolen from him, taking away his will to live.

My private hell that day, or stairway to heaven, was to stay there as long as it took, humbling myself to the nth degree. I put on the Red Sox cap, I lay down on the floor, I drank from his cup nestled under my armpit through a long straw, I gurgled like he did, I gesticulated wildly. I did everything in my power to be like him.

Nothing.

I went home shattered. The next day, in his bed, he lay there with his Red Sox cap on, drinking from a cup nestled under his armpit through a long straw. I swear to this day I saw a sparkle in his eye, a look of triumph, and more than a hint of forgiveness.

That day I started to become a pastor, not just a preacher, not just a know it all, tell it all, do it all, fill in the blank. He saved my career.

At one of our lay-led summer services, a woman in our church gave a superb sermon on "monkey hands and elephant ears." Drawing from her successful career in advertising, she talked about the tendency in her profession to always be doing something (monkey hands) rather than listening (elephant ears), and the problems that creates. I may not have known those terms at the time, but the CPE program, especially my Red Sox fan, was challenging me to move beyond the busyness of "monkey hands" to the outsized "elephant ears," more attuned to the world around me, the sounds, the smells, even the smallest incident.

My plan to save the church and change the world was built on plenty of work and lots of words, a busyness of hands and mouth. I intended to use my life to tell the world what's what, to use words, thousands of words, millions of words to end wars, fight injustice, save souls, fix problems. I would preach and teach and talk a blue streak until the world bent to my wisdom. That was the conceit of my generation, that we could "bull-session" our way to success.

That is how I began CPE. At the end of CPE we were asked to take a piece of paper, divide it in half. On one side we were told to draw a picture of what we had thought our ministry should be back when we started the program. On the other side we drew the image that represented what we now thought. On the left side I drew a gigantic mouth and a tiny, almost inconsequential ear. On the right side I drew a big ear — my "elephant ear" — and a tiny mouth. That began my transition from preacher to pastor.

The heart of pastoral care is a wonderfully descriptive verse from Paul's letter to the Romans, "weep with those who weep, rejoice with those who rejoice" (Romans 12:15). The whole chapter is an excellent job description for a pastor even though it applies to everyone. I tell my church members that the only difference between them and me is that I get paid to be a Christian, they don't, yet it is a fulltime job for all of us. Paul's advice is for all of us, but I take it to heart extra seriously as a pastor.

Wandering through Romans 12 certain verses, phrases, words stand out as central to pastoral ministry.

★ Offer your bodies as living sacrifices ...

★ do not conform to the pattern of this world ...

★ do not think more highly of yourself than you ought...

★ we have different gifts ...
★ do it cheerfully ...
★ love must be sincere ...
★ cling to what is good ...
★ be devoted to one another ...
★ honor one another above yourselves ...
★ never be lacking in zeal ...
★ keep your spiritual fervor, serving the Lord ...
★ be joyful in hope ...
★ be patient in affliction ...
★ be faithful in prayer ...
★ share with God's people in need ...
★ practice hospitality ...
★ live in harmony ...
★ do not be proud ...
★ be willing to associate with people of low position ...
★ do not be conceited ...
★ be careful to do what is right ...
★ live at peace with everyone ...
★ do not take revenge ...
★ overcome evil with good.

A Church that did that would be a great Church, a Christian who followed that would never have to worry about eternal life, and a pastor who took that on as a job description would have a most fulfilling career.

It is not a physically daunting list. Mostly it is about attitude and spirit, calling for humility, cheerfulness, sincerity, joy, restraint, harmony, caring. The most demanding command is to be persistent, whether in prayer or zeal or doing good. Among the joys of being a pastor is that you never know what each day will bring. To be a pastor is to be ever ready, and to be ever ready is to be persistent in attitude and spirit. Nestled within this sublime chapter is that superb summary of pastoral care. We are to "weep with those who weep, rejoice with those who rejoice." Sometimes it is that simple.

While serving a church in New York we were blessed one year to have many pregnancies, a delight for a small town church family. One by one each woman went into labor and returned home a few days later with what we all prayed for, a healthy baby.

The last of the women was in her early 40's, a surprise pregnancy. Unable to have children, she and her husband had adopted two babies who, by then, were teenagers. Hence, the surprise. Late one afternoon I got a phone call from the hospital. Our friend had given birth to a baby with Downs Syndrome and requested me to visit. Driving to the hospital I said a short prayer, "Lord, I haven't got the slightest idea what to say. You'll have to do this."

Our little church had enjoyed a string of happy, healthy births, including our own son; it had been week after week of joyful news. Now I had to visit a new mom and dad who had waited for the miracle of a lifetime. Instead, they were facing uncertainty, heartache, fear, not knowing what the future held for any of them.

I have no idea what I said. Believe me, if I could remember even a summary I would put it here as Exhibit A of pastoral care. The only memory I have is of my worry driving to see them. What I know is that a few weeks later, as we met to plan for the baby's baptism, the family credited that visit with making all the difference. They began to look at their baby, their family, their future, and each other in a new way.

I can't say whether I went that afternoon to weep with a family that was weeping, or to rejoice along with their rejoicing. It only seemed to matter that I was where they were.

It is not an original thought that showing up is half the battle. Brother Lawrence taught "Practicing the Presence of God," reminding us that presence, being fully present, is an art that can be practiced, learned and mastered.

One of the most intriguing miracle stories in the Gospels is one that happened through Jesus simply being present. Matthew 9 and Mark 5 tell us about a woman who had suffered from bleeding for twelve years despite the best efforts money could buy. She sought out Jesus because of his growing reputation as a holy man with healing powers, hoping only to get near enough to "touch the edge of his cloak" (Matthew 9:20). When she did, the Bible tells us that Jesus felt "virtue (or power) go out from him" (Mark 5:30, KJV). At that moment the bleeding stopped, the miracle happened, a healing took place — without Jesus even knowing. She came up behind him, touched only the hem (Matthew's version) or edge or fringe of his garment, almost a touch without touching. Jesus was not aware of her or her need, but he was there. In that lightest of encounters there was such power that Jesus felt something good, a virtue, flow from him to her. Pastoral care is often that simple, the power of presence, a sharing of virtue.

It is also true that often we do not know what good we do until long after, if at all. Raoul Wallenberg is one of my personal heroes, certainly a true hero of World War II. As a Swedish Envoy in Budapest he saved the lives of thousands of Jews, defying Eichmann face to face, braving the death that would catch up to him when the Soviets "disappeared" him. One of the Jews saved by Wallenberg said of him, "the thing about Wallenberg is that he came himself." That is the theology behind Jesus Christ. The idea of the incarnation is that God chooses to come himself, to become one with us, to enter into our daily life in a truly personal way, to be what the Christmas story calls our "Emmanuel — which means, 'God with us'" (Matthew 1: 23). Pastoral care is the human side of that divine touch, the choosing to be present in the midst of all the weepings and rejoicings of any day.

Being there is its own reward, but nevertheless gratitude is often expressed, even effusively. To respond by saying "it was nothing ... don't mention it ... aw, shucks" does not do justice to the gratitude. I finally found a better response, which is also truer. Alida and I always tell folks what an honor it is to be allowed into their lives. It is a precious privilege to be invited and welcomed into the most joyful and hurtful intimacies of daily life. Such is pastoral care.

The three P's: preaching, prayer and pastoral care. As a pastor, if you can't preach, don't pray, and won't visit, you are dead in the water. And the "tie that binds" all three together is love.

Early one morning on the steps of St. Giles' Church in Prague, near Old Town Square, I chatted with an elderly priest. He told me that he had been a priest for 'only' fifty-one years. God had called him into ministry in 1949, but the Communists had prevented him from serving as a priest until 1964. "The stories I can tell," he said, with a sparkle in his eye.

Not wanting to miss an opportunity, I asked, "What makes a good priest?" If anything, his eyes sparkled even more as he rattled off four bits of perfect advice: "Love God, of course. Love your people. Serve them. Teach them."

When I began writing this book, I asked my father the same question, and he was equally succinct, paraphrasing Jesus: "Love God with all you have, and love everybody else just as much" (Matthew 22:37-39).

Both of these pastors, in their nineties, with their entire careers lived in the turbulence of the last sixty years, see ministry as ultimately about Love.

The truth is that people go into ministry with many motives. To be a pastor of a Church, even today, is to be in a position of some power, some influence, some prestige and privilege, some security. People listen to you. You get to wear fancy robes, and use several titles. It can be a rush – for all the wrong reasons. And pastors going into ministry for that 'rush' are a good part of the reason that church buildings are being turned into apartments, restaurants, museums, and clubs.

Forget the power and go for the love. If Church is not a place where Love is central, there is no reason to be there. And if there is no reason to be there, people won't want to be there. So, love your church. Love your people.

Churches and pastors are filled with plenty of imperfections. We come up with an endless stream of bad ideas, bad programs, bad behaviors and bad leaders. Thankfully, the Bible reminds us that "love covers a multitude of sins" (1 Peter 4:8). That love cleanses and empowers. It takes away the stain of past failures and empowers the best efforts we put forward now.

A pastor who loves dearly will be loved dearly. That exchange of love empowers a pastor and a church to do more and to be more in ministry than they would otherwise dare. When I look back over my life's work, I have been afforded an amazing degree of freedom to explore and to experiment, to broaden, even to fail. Such freedom is birthed in love.

On a visit to Edinburgh years ago, I came across a young man in a park, standing on a 'soapbox,' preaching his heart out — by raging, attacking, yelling, threatening everyone around him. To my surprise I saw him again the next morning. He was at the local Baptist church, one of the congregation. It was a joyful, hopeful, quite loving church. What a contrast. On his own he gave people hell. But down deep, he wanted love.

EIGHT

The Last Enemy: Church Meets Death

"Our Savior Jesus Christ has destroyed death, and he has brought life and immortality to light." (2 Timothy 1:10)

Death is the Church's ultimate test, ultimate challenge, ultimate promise, and ultimate purpose. We are a people gathered around a very incredible idea that Jesus was put to death one Friday afternoon, and by Sunday morning Jesus was fully back to life. He was as dead as dead can be by every earthly definition. Then, suddenly, he was as alive as alive can be by every earthly definition.

That is why he is known as Jesus Christ, not just Jesus of Nazareth, or Jesus son of Joseph the carpenter. He did something with death that no one had ever done before, promising that this victory was only the "first fruits" (1 Corinthians 15:20) of a universe-wide, history-wide harvest of resurrection. This is what elevates Church beyond a philosophy, a teaching, a code of ethics, or any good thing that is not quite enough.

Jesus delivered the quite enough. That makes him the Christ.

Our faith in Christ gives us an incredible boldness in the face of the worst evils. Even death. Christ wants to help us soar above it. But death still packs a wallop that sets me back more than I want to admit.

The Book of Ecclesiastes is most famous for the passage in chapter three, a list of life's balances that we all face. "For everything there is a season, and a time for every matter under heaven," it begins, before contrasting life and death, war and peace, love and hate, sewing and rending. Each, it says, has its time. But death rarely comes to us as naturally as a change of season. Mostly death intrudes, disrupts, devastates.

I confess that as a pastor death often feels like a personal failure. On an intellectual level, I know that's silly. Yet on a feeling level each death challenges and hurts. After all, Christianity is built on the miracle of life. We begin with a miraculous birth and end with a miraculous resurrection, and everything in between is life-affirming.

Even in the midst of sickness, we continue to be hopeful and prayerful, yearning for death to be kept away. But we know it is inevitable. On one occasion, a person in our community became gravely ill, and one concerned friend suggested to another that a prayer service be held at Greenfield Hill. "Why?" that second friend responded. "Everyone that Greenfield Hill prays for dies." That, of course, is true. Our church is almost three hundred years old. Other than the folks alive today, every single person prayed for at Greenfield Hill Church in those three centuries has died. That is reality.

When I was a young pastor, a dear friend's mother was dying and I very consciously decided not to offer to make the trip to visit her. Why? Because I was afraid, and I did not want to fail. Even all these years later I am not sure if I did not want to fail her, or my friend, or myself. I just remember an awful sense of inadequacy, that I was newly minted in the Gospel of life and could do nothing about death, even for a friend. It was certain that my prayer would fail, I would fail, and death would win.

In the face of that Jesus said, "I am the way, the truth, and the life" (John 14:6). Fair enough. Great people think like that. Greatness almost requires a self-confidence bordering on arrogance. When Reggie Jackson joined the New York Yankees he referred to himself as "the straw that stirred the drink." He was going to mix things up and make things happen. We want our leaders to believe in themselves and in their ability to offer a way, truth, and life worth following.

But Jesus took it a huge step further when he declared, "I am the resurrection and the life" (John 11:25). That is more than a way to follow and a truth to believe in to make this life more manageable. It takes us to another world, literally. That is big. And, as St. Paul suggests, that is the basis for the greatest story ever told or else we are the biggest fools on earth to believe such a thing (1 Corinthians 15:14-19).

The central person of the Christian faith is Jesus. Whatever blends in harmoniously with Jesus I am interested in. Whatever does not, I am not interested. I did not arrive at this point lightly. Intellectually and practically I have explored the nooks and crannies and the main streets of most religious expressions of faith.

An opera singer I pastored was fervently devoted to Christ. She had spent years entering into the faith experiences of east and west, until ending up back home in the Protestant Congregationalism of her childhood, happy and satisfied with Christ. Like her, I no longer find myself looking at Jesus and wanting more.

Jesus is the central person, and the central message of the Christian faith is two-fold. You are loved. There is eternal life.

Or put it this way:

1. Jesus died for your sins.
2. Jesus rose from the dead.

The bottom line is the same. Because you are loved, you are forgiven. Because you are forgiven, there is resurrection for you. Biblically it comes out, "For God so loved the world, that he gave his only begotten Son, that whosoever believeth in him shall not perish, but have everlasting life" (John 3:16). In this extraordinary verse, God's motivation is love. God's action is Jesus. God's result is our eternal life. Eternal life is not an adjunct or secondary teaching; it shapes the living of this life. Some Christians have minimized this life by emphasizing eternal life's "pie in the sky, by and by." To the contrary, eternal life is meant to maximize this life, setting us free to live fully, boldly, daringly, faithfully, even sacrificially. The idea of heaven is meant to take away the "sting of death" (1 Corinthians 15:55-57), putting the death of this life in perspective. It does not take away sorrow or deny the great loss that comes with the end of a human life we hold dear. Instead, we are invited to see a larger picture that remains to be fulfilled, that awaits our participation, and that welcomes our presence when the time comes.

"Do not sorrow as those who have no hope" is Paul's realistic advice (1 Thessalonians 4:13). We are not forbidden to sorrow; we are invited not to be hopeless in our sorrow. Our sorrow is real, our loss is great, and heaven is also real and also great. This is not the end. This, and all we know, is not the sum and substance of our lives.

Dietrich Bonhoeffer was one of the true heroes of World War II. A German pastor, he was teaching at Union Seminary in New York City as the Nazis took control of Germany. Bonhoeffer chose to return to Germany and to use his Christian faith as a witness against Nazism. He eventually sacrificed his pacifism to take part in a plot to assassinate Hitler. When it failed he was arrested, and at the moment of his execution he perfectly summarized the Christian hope: "This is the end; for me, the beginning of life."

He was not cheapening his life by embracing the promise of eternal life. Instead, he enriched the value of life, including his own, through confidence in eternal life. This is not escapism. Bonhoeffer was able to hold together two powerful and paradoxical realities: life and how we live it; death, and what comes after it.

I am intrigued by death, not in a morbid or fearful way, and not so much by what it is as by how we face it. If it is something we all must do there must be a way to do it that makes the most of it. The lead-up to death, the process of dying, affects life much more than we can imagine. The eternal life of afterlife and the afterlife of the living are equally important.

Church must be at the heart of it all. Dying, death, and grieving, what happens to us when we are dead, and what happens to folks left behind, are at the heart of ministry. It may not seem it as we busy ourselves managing finances, property and program but ultimately the questions of life and death and beyond impact every soul of Church life.

Not surprisingly, the day by day process of dying is more worrisome for many than the prospects of afterlife. Obviously, most of my life is spent among people of faith, however small or undeveloped. Jesus so strongly affirmed the power of even the smallest grain of mustard seed size faith (Matthew 17:20) that our people readily accept some concept of eternity. It is a sort of given.

Dying, however, is very tangible, very personal, and very intimate. It is the most universal, inevitable unknown that we face, seemingly out of our control yet begging to be controlled.

If dying was more like turning off and on a light switch we could handle it more with grace and equanimity. Instead, dying more often feels like lurching about in the dark, looking for the light switch, bumping into things, afraid of falling down, grasping and reaching out, trying to get acclimated before, at last, we find the switch and everything that was scary or uncertain in the dark is now peaceful in the light.

The modern movement of euthanasia, "death with dignity" rights, and assisted suicide are our attempts to take control of the last intimate choice of life this side of heaven.

We have watched dying be taken over by medicine. Advances in medical technology have moved faster than our conversations about ethics and end of life decisions.

During the 2009 debate over the Affordable Care Act ("ObamaCare"), a number of people were angered by the provision that would offer reimbursement to doctors for having end-of-life discussions with their patients. Their opposition devolved into angry shouts about "death panels." Some feared that the government would determine who could get what care as life's prospects dimmed. But as the war of words raged on, I was one who was rooting for the original idea: that doctors should start to initiate such end of life discussions as part of their professional practice.

I have been in the middle of these discussions my whole career, often as the initiator, and am honored to do so. To do so in partnership with doctors would be the best of both worlds. Sadly, pastors are often pushed out of the loop. Privacy laws, hospital policies and a general sidelining of clergy make it more difficult to pastor exactly at the point where pastoral care is urgently needed. I am old enough and obstinate enough to push my way through the roadblocks, and once I break through I am always warmly welcomed by the patient, the family, and the medical staff. After all, we are in this together. People want a faith perspective as surely as they seek a medical perspective and the perspective of family. The role of Church is to bring the hope of faith into the darkest corners of our lives.

This is crucial at a time when people feel they are losing all control in the mayhem of dying. People used to talk about letting nature take its course, or allowing God's will to happen. Today, nature and God's will get trumped by technology, by well-meaning EMTs, ICUs, doctors and family members who choose to fight for our every breath. Yet the more we visit loved ones in nursing homes and hospitals, and the more we see life extended and dying extended along with it, the more we fear it. What was designed to help too often adds to the hurt.

Yet dying is inevitable. In my career I have pastored over ten thousand people, going through everything imaginable with them, guiding, counseling, and hoping for all manner of outcomes. But the only thing I can guarantee is death, and the dying that comes before it.

We can all wish for our dying to be "in a moment, in the twinkling of an eye," as St. Paul imagined the transition from this life to the next (1 Corinthians 15:52), but it is more likely to be a long, slow slog from robust health to decrepitude — and doesn't that sound attractive. The modern art of dying has lost the art, leaving us with only modern dying. This offers hospice and palliative care at one end, and the heroics of science at the other end. Both are to be admired, and I have tremendous personal gratitude for each. The relief from pain is a miracle in itself, and the efforts of medicine to extend life are equally miraculous.

A gentleman took me to dinner to confide that he had been given a dire diagnosis. Together, we arrived at a plan. As long as he wanted to fight for life I would stand with him, advocating on his behalf with family and friends who might be urging him to let go and not suffer. When he had had enough I would stand with him, advocating on his behalf with those who might not be ready to let him go. He would grab the benefits of science as long as he could, and then settle into the arms of compassion when it was time. Interestingly, it was his commitment to faith and Church that encouraged him both to fight on and then to let go. Faith informed both, Church enveloped both.

The role of Church is to embody the best of our faith every day. In any given year we face the full range of deaths: the death of dreams, of careers, of marriages, of friendships, of homes, of health, and of life. To every experience of death we bring the same message of faith, which is resurrection. Church must embody resurrection in all its fullness. As we study the scriptural promise of eternal life we read of reunion, of life beyond regrets and mistakes and plain old sin, of an eternity of love empowered by forgiveness, of "no more tears" (Revelation 7:17). To embody such faith means to bring it to the sickbed, the hospice care, the funeral, the graveside, and to the grieving. To embody it means that every time someone turns to the Church they can see it; they don't have to hunt for it or ask for it. It is us. We are an Easter people, and we should look like it, act like it, and sound like it. We must live Resurrection. Every death deserves such hope.

None of this is to suggest that it is easy. Dying is not just work, it is hard work. Death is brutal in its finality. Grieving is raw. To that brutal, raw, hard work the Church chooses to bring not an alternate reality but a parallel reality. We do not deny dying, death and grieving their power, but we do not give them the final word.

Since dying in some form and death itself are inevitable, why not remove as much anxiety, uncertainty and fear as possible? This does not mean walking around thinking about your death all the time. Quite the opposite, the result of good planning is to be able to think about other stuff. If your life is in order, your affairs are in order, your relationships and loves are in order, your faith is in order, and your wishes are known, then you have done all in your power to allow life to end as serenely as possible.

To get there requires intentionality, to intentionally look deep at your life and your faith, to note clearly your pluses and minuses. Lent exists for this very purpose. The idea of Lent is to give folks a forty-day period to assess themselves and it is not a coincidence that Lent begins with Ash Wednesday.

The placing of a mark of ash on the forehead has long been a staple of Roman Catholic piety, and we now embrace it enthusiastically at our church. We are a quintessential New England Congregational church, a small, white, wooden box, no ornamentation or color or statues or stained glass. We are beautifully and exquisitely plain. It can be powerful, dramatically so, to introduce a little ritual or symbolism into the heart of Pilgrim plainness and piety. Ash Wednesday has become important to us. We use the ashes as a blunt reminder of our own mortality, echoing the Biblical promise of "ashes to ashes, dust to dust.... from dust we came, to dust we shall return" (Ecclesiastes 3:20; 12:7; Anglican Book of Common Prayer).

Lent begins with a reminder of death, of dying and decay, of mortality. Churches then use Lent to mirror Jesus' wilderness experience when he was tempted and tested and pushed by the devil. The devil tried to cheapen Jesus' life, weaken his resolve, and mock his mission. Jesus used those forty days, his own little Lent, to put his own life and death in balance, to assess himself, to put together a plan for life that took note of death (Matthew 4:1-11). The message of our Church is that if Jesus thought it worth doing, maybe we should. The idea of giving up something for Lent, and, conversely, taking something up, is a kind of lightweight attempt at life assessment, but it is a step. It is a way of admitting that there is something in our life that needs fixing, by addition or subtraction. The mortality symbol of ash and the repentance symbol of some behavioral change are the start of a plan.

One Lent it occurred to me that the great Good News of Easter might be louder and clearer if we looked at death even more starkly. In many Protestant churches we happily greet Jesus on Palm Sunday and rejoice in resurrection on Easter, but we skip the harsh reality of suffering, dying and death in between. We no more want to imagine Jesus going through all that than we do for ourselves and our loved ones. Dying and death are better out of sight and out of mind. But for one Lent we hit them both head on in sermons and discussions.

Drawing heavily from my pastoral experiences, I also found two books immensely helpful, *At the Hour of Death* by Philippe Aries and *The Art of Dying* by Rob Moll.[23] Both recall a time when dying and death were truly community events of interest to one and all. They reminded me that we could actually participate proactively in the process in ways that would make it better. To over simplify, we can decide how we would like to go about dying, and do it.

This has nothing to do with method. It is not a matter of moving to Oregon, joining the Hemlock Society, or looking for Dr. Kevorkian's notes. It is about awareness. We are mortal; we are all in the process of dying, so why not take the steps now that put us more at peace when our dying becomes more active, so to speak, more urgent?

I remember visiting two elderly women in the same week who had entirely different approaches. One lived in an elegant home, and as I sat for tea I noticed a white piece of paper attached to every single item in the house, from the humblest lamp to the most precious antique. Written on each paper was the name of the person she was giving the item to after her death. She did this years in advance so that together they could enjoy the bequeathing, imagine its new setting, talk about its history and use. She told me that this gave her immense joy and wonderful peace of mind.

The other lady was a sadder story. Her doctor had informed her that she was dying, and she wanted me to arrange reconciliation with her daughter. Her daughter had

---

[23] Aries, Philippe. *At the Hour of Death*. Knopf Doubleday Publishing Group, 2008. Moll, Rob. *The Art of Dying*. InterVarsity Press, 2010.

married a "black man" a dozen years before, she had boycotted the wedding, had not seen them since, nor her grandchildren born to them.

Now, after a dozen years of hurtful silence, I was expected to arrange a happy gathering around her lovely death bed among her fluffed pillows, setting aside years of bigotry and overcoming genuine ignorance. She wanted a rosy reunion with a son-in-law and grandchildren she had never met or even acknowledged. While she was demanding that I do this, and expecting it to happen, it was clear that to me that she was full of fear. With her life slipping away, she faced her end with fear, regret, and bitterness about life's choices, hers and others', and their consequences.

What if, perhaps six years before, this dear lady had recognized her mortality, even if it was not yet knocking on her door? What if, in that day of enlightenment, full of vim and vigor, she had dialed the phone herself? Or better yet, taken the subway to her daughter's apartment, surprised her and her husband with a warm embrace, and met her grandchildren with a gentle and kind spirit? In an afternoon of humility and grace she could have set aside lost years, restored her family, and given a gift of joy to be treasured through her final breath.

Death is always pending. Good genes, good luck, timing, God's will and modern medicine may keep death from being just around the corner but it is still over the next hill, up around the bend, or somewhere down the road. Our challenge is to know that when death is ready for us, we are ready for death.

Our family faith roots are in a small denomination called Advent Christian, which emphasizes the imminent return (second coming) of Christ. Even more than the average person anticipates that death will come someday, the average Advent Christian anticipates Christ's return inevitably and imminently, ending life as we know it. In terms of daily existence, that is not much different than death. Whichever way it happens, a fatal heart attack or Christ's return, either way this life ends and the next begins.

Once, while visiting my Advent Christian grandfather, Linwood, I found him gazing off into the distance. "What are you thinking about, Grandpa?" I asked. "Eternity," he said matter-of-factly, "what else is there?" That was said declaratively, as if it were obvious. Christ's return would start our eternity and that is just as possible in the next instant as death.

There is a saying that comes out of such Advent Christian "second coming" theology which is useful to everyone: we should believe that Jesus is coming again soon, and live as though he is never coming again. We should live as if Jesus awaits us there and then, and needs us here and now. We should, paradoxically, live in such a way that we are always prepared and yet always surprised. Live fully, to the last moment, a life of faith and a life of life. This is the role of Church and pastor in the ongoing reality of dying.

I wrote much of this chapter during and just after a visit to Venice. Other than canals, gondolas and great food, Venice is rich with the giants of Italian classic art: Titian, Tintoretto, Veronese, and colleagues. Their art emerged from the time of plagues ravaging Europe, only adding to the woes of daily life already lived on the edge of death. All of this is reflected in their art. The splendor of heaven, the reward of faith, and the omnipresence of miracle emerge triumphantly over the world of suffering, horror and unrelenting dying. God's eternity trumps earth's depravity. My grandfather was right.

Meanwhile, we still have to die.

The books by Aries and Moll offer the wisdom of the ages. Since people have been dying forever it may well be that the ages have a lot to teach us. We don't have to go back far, or far away, to find a time when dying and death were a community event, something entered into fully by family and neighbors. People came in and out of the house, meals were organized, neighbors took a collection, people stopped on the sidewalk when a funeral procession went by, visiting hours and even funerals took place in the parlor, faith was front and center through it all from last rites to church cemeteries.

Aries refers to "the Tame Death" and Moll to "the Art of Dying." Both offer the prospect of taking something that appears to be out of control, disruptive, disturbing, messy, and frightening and bring to it a measure of order and peace. It is not impossible, but dying is work and we should welcome that. Just about anything you have done well in your life that you are proud of, anything that represents you at your best, took work. Why not apply the same work ethic, the same pride of work, to the final measure of your life?

Moll states that everyone has four things they need to say to someone:

1. Please forgive me.
2. I forgive you.
3. Thank you.
4. I love you.

All four can be specific or general, but each one gets you thinking and brings you closer. Closer is near to the word "closure", the popular word for what we all hope for when death comes. Being closer may well be the closure we seek, and if we can have it well in advance of death, all the better for everyone. Whether you do it face to face or in a YouTube video or in your head or to God in a prayer, it starts a powerful conversation. The idea is to clear the deck, do away with regrets, and set yourself free not just to die but to live more fully until you die. That is the only way to face any future, even eternity. No baggage.

Moll's *The Art of Dying* puts it in more formal, classic terms taken from centuries of Christian practice.

1. Acknowledge what's happening: dying.

2. Recollect what is important.

3. Ask forgiveness.

4. Offer your final thoughts and encouragements.

5. Express your faith in Christ and in eternal life.

6. Take your leave.

7. Commend yourself and your loved ones to God.

Does that seem like a lot? Well, yes. Therefore, two things. First, don't wait until your final breath — you shouldn't cut it that close. And, second, it really takes work.

What Moll's list is getting at is the need to be honest with yourself, loving with others, confident in your faith, and trusting of God. There is no glossing it over, no sugar coating it, no short cuts, which may explain why so many avoid most, if not all, of the steps. So many people cannot tackle what Step 1 requires (acknowledgment); therefore numbers 4 and 7 are not likely to happen. I have known good people who easily grasped the faith-based concepts of numbers 5 and 7, but found 1 through 4 too personal. Others, comfortable with the personal, are uncomfortable with overt statements of faith, however real it may be inside them. As for number 3, we pray for forgiveness every Sunday in the Lord's Prayer as a sort of ecclesiastical group hug. But at one's weakest, to choose to look another in the eye and dredge up old hurts — well, that is tough.

Death takes work. But good work is its own reward. How's that for good old American, Horatio Alger, Protestant work ethic?

I'll say it: I hate death. While writing this I realize what a strange mix of beliefs I hold. I believe in euthanasia and I am grateful for modern science and medicine. I believe in heaven in all its glory. Yet I treasure this life.

I hate death because of what it does on this side of heaven. No amount of heaven replaces the loss of a loved one now. Through all these pages I have purposely not mentioned my mother. All who know me realize that the death of my mother impacted me more devastatingly than anything else in my life. My mother lived a wonderful life. She was a truly good person, a true help-mate as a wife, a perfect mother and grandmother, and a woman of profound faith. After a fast-moving cancer took hold of her, she died with a minimum of suffering at the age of sixty-six. Other than too soon, all in all it was a wonderful life. At her death God's arms opened wide, heaven rejoiced, and she is fine. I believe all of that, one hundred percent.

And yet still I grieve, almost thirty years later. Heaven is not a replacement for life; it is a reward for life. In truth, I honor sorrow. A friend of mine lost her young adult son, and in her sorrow other friends advised her to get a prescription for some pills so she would feel better. She told me, "I don't want to feel better. I don't want to take a pill. I lost my son. It should hurt." I agreed with her.

Her sorrow was honorable.

Certainly, there are people whose sorrow is paralyzing and destructive, a downward spiral into an abyss of despair and loneliness. There is also a sorrow that is a measure of love, a fact of life, a wound that endures privately. Life and love and faith and friendships and work and fun all continue. They, we, are not frozen in time, not to be pitied. We don't need a pill. It is just that the grief is still stricken, the heart is still broken. The sorrow is still full.

"Blessed are they that mourn," Jesus said, surely startling his listeners. And then he added "for they shall be comforted" (Matthew 5:4). Both are true: the one now, and the other later. The later comes in different ways at different times, offering comfort if we are open to it.

Art and faith came together one Good Friday at my church to give to me what the Bible calls "the peace which passeth all understanding" (Philippians 4:7). Our very Protestant, New England, low key Congregational church does Good Friday in a big way. We have a "Stations of the Cross" service at noon, and in the evening we hold a Tenebrae Service. After a hymn and sermon, the sanctuary is transformed by a blend of choral music and scripture readings by our Deacons. As the choir sings, and the story is told, one by one candles on the altar are extinguished, and lights dimmed, until, at the point of Jesus's death, we are entombed in darkness.

In that darkness of this particular Tenebrae service, two of our church musicians, cellist Niles Luther and pianist Barbara Mayer, began to play Max Bruch's "Kol Nidrei", based on the classic Jewish song of the dead. Long, slow, mournful, passionate, haunting, and lovely. Everything we fear about death, and hope, and feel was alive in those moments.

I sat immersed in my private sorrow, choosing that night to think hard about my mother, a focus I mostly avoid for the pain. I can't shake the sorrow, but I can avoid the pain. But this night my mother spoke to me. My mother was Swedish, so we are not given to drama or effusiveness. We live life with a determined balance. With that sort of quiet, straight-forward Swedish demeanor my mother assured me that she was fine. God is there, she promised, heaven is wonderful, we will be together again, stop worrying, and enjoy life. Then my mother returned to her place, and me to mine next to Alida, in our church, art and faith granting me a glimpse of heaven.

Faith is a choice. I choose to believe that what I just described really happened. I choose to believe in God, Jesus, the Virgin Birth, Easter, heaven, resurrection, and grace. There is not much proof for any of that. Faith is a choice based on a variety of factors; the same ones that convince me may leave another quizzical. But it is my choice to live my life through the world view of faith.

Some of it I picked up on my own, some I experienced, some I need, and some I borrowed from others. A favorite professor told me that, often with faith, we look to people whom we trust. We have found them truthful and reliable on things we could prove. Then, when they come along and tell us something unlikely, impossible, incredible, unprovable, do we abandon them, or mock them? Or take them at their word, on faith? In my life I have been blessed with several key people whom I know would not steer me wrong. Even about the impossible.

Another great man, Dr. Henry Mitchell, on a trip we took to Africa together, was telling me about the power of mothers and faith. He said, "When you have a choice between what your Momma told you and what the Preacher told you, you go with your Momma." He later went on to put other authority figures in place of the preacher, like a politician, a boss, a friend, all in contrast to your mother. "Go with your Momma," Henry said.

My mother told me that there is a heaven. That is enough for me.

Getting Into Heaven: Through the Eyes of St. Agnes (1 Thessalonians 4:13-18)

I got in!
Sin or no sin
I really got in

I've arrived
survived
truth to tell
I squeaked by hell
But I'm in.
I look around
heaven's lost and found
folks coming through the door
surprised to be on the other shore
some still angry
some amazed
some disappointed
perhaps disjointed
a few still wired
a few just tired

a little panic
a little frantic
looking for someone
long gone
who left them alone

Then slowly it dawns
what we've heard about
for so long
and now that we're here
and joy is squeezed from fear
we realize
we have arrived –
alive!

And, yes,
as I wander and wonder
there's more than a few I'm surprised to see

not as many, perhaps,
as surprised to see me. [24]

---

[24] Rowe, David Johnson, *"Getting Into Heaven."* In *Fieldstones of Faith, Vol. II.*
Inspired by a video art installation, Mark Wallinger's "Threshold to the Kingdom"

NINE

Mission

I played basketball in a rural village, Nsona Mpangu, in Bas Zaire, the lower part of what is now the Congo. To my amazement the game was mostly played in the air, pinpoint passes from player to player up and down the dirt court. It was more like aerial soccer than the basketball of my New York City youth where we were all asphalt legends. In my days everybody dribbled, fancy dribbles, off beat dribbles, between the legs dribbles, spinning and weaving, we even called it "show time."

Not in old Zaire. All of a sudden I could see basketball with fresh eyes, the flow and movement, even the beauty of the game. Not a one-on-one spectacle of individuality but an intricate design of community. It was an "aha" moment.

Mission has provided me with more "aha" moments than any other activity of my life. Somehow, glimpsing life through the prism of elsewhere helps me to see everything more clearly. Priorities, time, relationships, nationhood, citizenship, church life, evangelism, neighborliness, forgiveness, history, health, infrastructure, travel, faith all come into sharper focus in a fresh environment.

Books and films do the same. They give us a chance to look at issues from a distance and with a perspective that provides clearer understanding than when we are looking at something that is too close and personal. We can take what we learn outside our comfort zone and bring it home, put it to use.

Take politics. It has been said that "democracy is the worst form of government, but it is better than any other." Aspects of American politics and democracy drive me crazy. There is plenty of free speech I am tempted to shut up. But my mission travels have taken me to places where rights have been curtailed, the press muted or silenced, free speech has a heavy price, clergy have been killed and churches destroyed.

On my third trip to Uganda, the second after the fall of their dictator, Idi Amin, all of a sudden there were newspapers everywhere. Laid out along the sidewalks were newspapers of every kind, size, color and opinion. People gawked and grabbed, tussled over copies, clutched them preciously to their chest, showed them proudly to strangers. All of a sudden my complaint about excesses and abuses of American public discourse seemed petty. Those folks on the streets of Kampala knew how precious even bad words and stupid words are. In so many things, what I take for granted on my own soil is treated as priceless on foreign soil. I need those reminders.

Travel is a good example. My mission travels began in the mid-1970s with an extensive journey that crisscrossed Africa. It opened me to a world where you lived by faith, open to every change, unfazed by any delay or cancellation. That is not how I live my daily life in the U.S. of A. Here I want my planes to land on time, my trains to run on time, people to show up on time. I expect regularity and dependability and order. When it doesn't happen I quickly make myself miserable, and those around me even more miserable. I whine and complain and seethe, and question God's will. I never imagine any good coming from something not working out just the way I had planned.

In the world of mission I suspend all that anxiety over schedule and plans and time, perfectly at ease to "let go and let God." In Hebrews 11:1 the Bible teaches that "faith is being sure of what we do not know, and certain of what we cannot see." In the mission field I simply assume that the unseen and the unknown are precisely what God wants me to see and know. On a practical level that means knowing that a full day of events that has just been cancelled will inevitably lead to activities and encounters (the unseen and the unknown) of great importance and value. The end result is that I have never spent a bad day in the mission field.

I assume that each experience will be wonderfully adventurous and spiritually instructive. Delays, cancellations, obstacles, unexpected changes and serendipitous events are welcomed as part of God's master plan. There is a greater sense of God's bottom line at work than my own. Things become clearer theologically, practically, professionally, personally, Biblically. Christianity has a long history of complicating the basics. The mission field has a way of un-complicating the basics.

I once met a man called 'The Fire Tender.' Back in the 1980s my friend, Paul Davis, and I took our youth groups to work on Habitat for Humanity's first truly hardcore urban project. We were renovating a six-story apartment house on the Lower East Side of Manhattan, an area known as 'Alphabet City,' as Avenues A, B, C and D run through it. Alphabet City then resembled a war zone. Rubble everywhere; drugs, crime, and poverty permeating every inch.

Onto that barren landscape stepped the Fire Tender. He took over an empty lot, hauled in scrap wood, set up a small bonfire, put on a huge kettle, and dumped in every bit of food he could scrounge — creating his own "stone soup." Just like Jesus, the Fire Tender fed the multitudes by taking what seemed not enough and making it into plenty. Twenty hours a day the Fire Tender and his wife fed all comers, hundreds of hungry souls, with nonstop coffee and soup.

One winter we split up our Habitat work team of teenagers, sending half of them each day to help the Fire Tender. There were hours of slicing and dicing, cooking and cleaning, and good-natured banter with all the eaters and helpers and newfound friends. During some down time I found myself alone with the Fire Tender. I wanted to learn from him, pick his brains, take away some deep spiritual insight that would shape the rest of my life. So, I asked him what led him to do this work, what inspired him? As I awaited his profound answer, ready to engrave it in my mind as a holy mantra, the Fire Tender made a sweeping motion with his arm, pointing in all directions. "Isn't it obvious?" he asked.

That really is mission, doing the obvious for those who are overlooked. This is our FOCI/Azariah theology: "see a need, meet a need." Jesus' words were just as simple: "feed the hungry, visit the lonely, clothe the naked" (Matthew 25:34-36).

I have learned more about being a church, being a pastor, being a Christian from mission experiences than anywhere else. This is not to say that the same lessons were not available closer to home, only that the lessons from mission got my attention louder and clearer. Justice, mercy, sacrifice, ritual, worship, marriage, pastoral care, theology, even scripture, take on a power, a clarity, and an urgency when I experience them outside my comfort zone front door.

I made two trips to Uganda after its Civil War led to the overthrow of Idi Amin. During those visits there was nothing that went as planned. From arrival to departure every day was disrupted. When I arrived the first time with a small Habitat for Humanity team we found a nation in chaos and the capital, Kampala, dysfunctional. The Intercontinental Hotel had no food and no water. At night there was gunfire all around. During the day appointments weren't kept, meetings didn't meet, people didn't show up, arrangements weren't arranged. Every road trip was on a wing and a prayer, minus the wing. Road blocks, flat tires, rebels and soldiers demanding bribes were on every day's agenda.

And yet....

And yet these were among the most profound experiences of my life. At every turn I was given a Ph.D. level course in Bible, gratitude, community, resilience, theology, Church.

At one village in the north of Uganda every man, woman, and child came out to greet us upon our arrival. During the welcome ceremony they presented us with a goat and some grains. These were people who had lost everything in the decade of Amin's genocide against his own people, especially in the north. These villages had nothing, and from their nothingness they managed to conjure up a goat to give as a "thank you" to a group of well-heeled Americans.

One morning I met with a large group of widows whose husbands had been killed by Amin's soldiers. I expressed great admiration and surprise at their determination and joy after all they had endured. They then expressed greater surprise at my surprise, reminding me that I was a pastor supposedly well acquainted with the Bible. "Don't you know your Bible?" they asked. "Don't you know the story of Daniel in the Lion's Den, of Shadrach, Meshach, Abednego in the fiery furnace? We are Daniel. We are Shadrach, Meshach, and Abednego. We have been in the lion's den. We have come out of the fiery furnace!" (Daniel 3; Daniel 6)

From the comfort of my own life it is easy to assume that the miseries of others are too daunting, too overwhelming, too horrific to be endured with any measure of grace or equanimity or faith. When I put myself in their shoes I imagine lying down and giving up just like the old prophet Elijah. We often say, "I could never do that ... I could never get through that ... I couldn't handle that." The prophet Elijah seemed to agree at a certain low point in his career. He was rejected, hated, threatened, pursued. His entire life seemed a waste, a failure, and he was ready to quit on God and on life.

In 1 Kings 19:3-8 it is written that "Elijah was afraid" and declared to God, "I have had enough, Lord. Take my life." The Bible reports that God would not give up on Elijah, sending an angel to stir him up, strengthen him, even feed him, and push him onward.

All across the mission field I have met people who, like Elijah, had every reason to be afraid, and every right to say to God, "I have had enough." But they don't do that. And we sometimes sell ourselves short by thinking that, if confronted by the same horrors, we would lie down like Elijah and pray to die. Chances are we would not; we would surprise ourselves with the very same resilience shown by the poor, the troubled, the oppressed all over the world. What has humbled me is to see so clearly that their resilience is rooted in faith. I should know that in my world. I do know that in their world.

As a young pastor I was nearly anti-mission. Like so many clergy I viewed mission as a competitor, taking money from our church budget and sucking up my people's time. I often threw away appeals, or chose not to bring mission needs before my church. Fortunately, an old time Baptist minister took me aside and said, "You know, it takes a lot of gall on your part to sit in your office and decide for other people what they should give to or not. Give them every mission opportunity you can, give them the chance. You'll be amazed at what it does for them and for your church." He was absolutely right.

Turning mission into a personal, self-improvement journey was probably not Jesus' intent for us when he issued his "Great Commission." But sometimes it's those smaller motivations which move us toward the larger purpose.

The Great Commission, Matthew 28:18-20, was the culmination of an extraordinary month in Jesus' life. In short order he had been celebrated, arrested, tortured, executed and buried. He is resurrected from the dead, spends time convincing friends that he is alive, then ascends to heaven. His last words became the foundation, the rationale for the so-called "mission work" of the Church: "Go ye into all the world ... baptizing... and teaching all that I have commanded."

Acts 1:8 expands on the idea, adding that we are to be his "witnesses from Jerusalem to Judea to the ends of the earth." With this Great Commission as its marching orders, the Church has stridden steadfastly into every community.

Mission and Evangelism are two sides of the same coin. They both push our efforts and our faith outward. They are at once the most important, most unpopular, most necessary, and most controversial parts of being Church. In Christian terms, all the 'evangel' words (evangelism, evangelical, evangelist) refer to sharing the 'Good News' – the literal translation of the word *evangelos* in the New Testament's original Greek. An evangelist is a person who shares the Good News of Jesus Christ, evangelism is the act of sharing it, and evangelical refers to people and churches who emphasize it. In the same vein, mission is a purpose, a task. A missionary is one who bears the purpose, does the task.

Americans are almost full-time evangelists. In secular terms, evangelism is the art of salesmanship, of believing enough in something to want others to know about it. If we have a great meal at a restaurant, we tell everyone about it. If we see a terrific movie, read an inspiring book, or go to a moving play, we slip it into every conversation, whether or not it's on topic to do so. During political campaigns, even the fussiest people put up lawn signs and add bumper stickers to their cars, boldly proclaiming the candidate who will be "good news" for the country. At the drop of a hat we will push our opinion or our experience of the best new diet, yoga center, gym, car or new piece of technology.

But many American Christians draw the line at talking about faith. We shy away from pushing the 'Good News' of Jesus Christ. What a loss.

At any one moment, half the world is walking around burdened by some sin, done by them or to them. And much of the world is suffering the effects of death, either heartbroken by the death of a loved one or worried about their own. Yet we would rather share news about a good book or restaurant than share help for grief or sin.

The reason is simple. Evangelism by evangelists from evangelical churches has presented the 'evangel' – the Good News – badly, poorly, and mean-spiritedly. We have used fear, intimidation, manipulation, deceit, group pressure, threats, all in pursuit of a noble goal, allegedly: to save souls. Lost in translation has been the spirit of our Spirit. As a result we now have honest-to-goodness, Bible-believing, God-loving Christians who are deeply hesitant about doing evangelism and mission. And we have broken, needy, hungry, searching people who are hesitant to look to Christianity for help. Again, what a loss.

Two comments helped me to put evangelism into perspective as a pastor. One of my seminary professors, Gabe Fackre, taught me that "evangelism is just one hungry person saying to another hungry person, 'Hey, I know where there is food.'" The power of that saying, and of that kind of evangelism, is in its humility. There is no master/servant, top/down, saved/unsaved dimension to that story. Both people are hungry. Both get to eat. The only difference is that one knows where the food is, and together they go to be nourished. Together.

The other comment came from my first visit to India. Our host was Bishop Sam Ponniah of the Church of South India, Diocese of Vellore. The churches under his care were thriving, precisely because evangelism permeated his vision of mission.

It was not a specialized activity, or event, or sideshow. It was as essential to everyday ministry as breathing is to everyday life. His comment to me was his own official motto: "Every Bishop a pastor; every pastor an evangelist." Or as the Apostle Paul and Nike both put it: "Just Do It!"

One afternoon Bishop Ponniah took me to a remote village. There, by the side of the road, was a most beautiful church. He had worked closely with an architect to create a space for worship that incorporated meaningful and clear aspects of Hinduism, Buddhism, Islam and Christianity. It was an arms-wide-open welcome to all who passed by, an invitation to know God right there, a place of no barriers, literally and figuratively.

Too much of evangelism's Good News has been wrapped in Bad News. Ponniah and Fackre, Halík and Azariah and my father, all the folks who have taught me and led me and mentored me in ministry, have carefully wrapped the Good News in Good News.

Mission defines Church. Invariably it shows us at our best and our worst. Our greatest accomplishments and our greatest blunders, our greatest heroics and our greatest follies, our greatest triumphs and our greatest defeats have been on the mission field.

My guess is that much of what Americans know about mission comes from Barbara Kingsolver's book *The Poisonwood Bible*, about missionaries in the old Belgian Congo as it emerged into independent Zaire. Her missionaries are foolhardy, arrogant, manipulative, bigoted, naïve, myopic, ignorant, dangerous, insensitive, and other adjectives I have forgotten. Kingsolver is right on target. World mission has been full of those adjectives acting as nouns, misrepresenting the Gospel in a thousand ways.

While attending a World Book Fair in New Delhi, India I was confronted by an author hawking his own anti-American, anti-Christianity, anti-mission books. First, he grabbed me and ranted about all the evils done by missionaries in the name of Christianity, mostly using my own list of adjectives. Then, as I grew weary of his rant, and skeptical, he opened up his book to show quotes and sources from missionaries' own writings, official reports and their letters back home, their books and biographies proving the very charges he was shouting. We have been greedy, chauvinistic, nationalistic, racist, opportunistic control freaks in our mission history. True enough.

My problem with Barbara Kingsolver and with the anti-missionary author at the Book Fair is that they both speak truth, but not enough truth. They miss both the majority of the story and the best part of the story. Mission is also done by people who are selfless, sacrificial, humble, unassuming, with hearts as big as all outdoors. Forget my adjectives and go to St. Paul's list of what he calls, "the fruits of the Spirit." He is saying that if you are a Christian, if God's spirit is at home in you, if you are a spiritual person by that definition, you will exhibit certain "produce." As certainly as an orange tree will produce an orange, we will produce these "fruits of the spirit: love, joy, peace, patience, kindness, goodness, faithfulness, gentleness and self-control" (Galatians 5:22-23).

In my experience the mission field produces these fruits in abundance and, in fact, they are the only way to do mission.

One year I led a Habitat work camp to India. We did ten days of hard work under a boiling sun, helping to build houses with poor villagers, followed by a week of cultural touring. Our family stayed on in Calcutta to visit Mother Teresa's "Mission-aries of Charity" and their work. It was profound, moving, even beautiful, despite the desperation of each loving act.

Mother Teresa's approach to mission is a good model for Church: always open to a new challenge. She became a nun to serve God, leaving her home world of Albania to study in a foreign country, Ireland. They sent her to serve in Calcutta, in a girls' school. This was back in the 1930s and 1940s, a time of deprivation and turmoil. One would think that she was fulfilling her vow of Christian missionary service. Yet God wanted more from her, daring her to leave what little she had in order to seek the presence of Christ in the lives of the truly poorest of the poor. This began the work for which she became a Saint. Mission can do for the Church what Mother Teresa's second calling did for her, take us deeper in meaning and purpose and practice. Church life, by itself, is important, vital, urgent. Mission sharpens it all.

Most profoundly I remember her Home for the Dying in Calcutta (now Kolkata). In a nation of extreme poverty, inequality, and the explosive social dynamics of urbanization — especially as India was at that time — the dying poor are often the most vulnerable. They have nothing and nobody, and their final fate may be a slow death abandoned on pavement. These became Mother Teresa's guests in a simple, clean, dignified place to face the end of life.

If I were to add "in the embrace of God's love" you would assume it to be allegorical or figurative, not literal. I saw the embrace of God's love literally. On a cot in the far room lay a young man. Gaunt, still, near death, he was about twenty-five but looked ninety-five, and his very long too-short life of suffering was soon to end. He was cradled in the arms of a young German, about the same age, but the perfect image of youth: hardy and healthy, ruggedly athletic, brimming with endless energy and boundless faith. The German boy spoke soothingly to the Indian boy, gently stroking his hair, touching his face, occasionally bending over to hug him. The young Indian never took his eyes off the German, as if he knew that life and love and God were all tied together in their mystical union. That is not overwrought writing, it is true to that moment. God and those two young men were accomplishing something together.

After some time had passed I said to the young German, "Thank you for what you are doing for him." He reached down to more fully embrace the Indian into almost a cuddle, looking with such love into his eyes, and without taking his eyes off him he corrected me, "Thank him for what he is doing for me."

There you have mission, in that one moment. From Mother Teresa's decision in Albania to become a nun, to her accepting assignment to Calcutta, to her deepened call to the poor, to bringing the dying in off the streets, to a young German taking a few weeks of summer fun to go and serve, to the openness of a dying Indian to receive love with such grace, to the people around the world who funded and prayed and cared — this is mission.

I do think that Jesus had that in mind as he gave his "Great Commission" to the disciples, urging them forever outward. Sometimes, more often than most of the world admits, it is a truly great commission. As a bonus, doing mission may well indeed be a personal, self-improvement journey that includes a three way mystical union. That is definitely imbuing mission with deep meaning, high expectations and profound purpose. Yet we make it more complicated than need be.

One afternoon I walked into a McDonald's, and while ordering my QuarterPounder I noticed a "Mission Statement" on the wall. In direct language they promised me a decent burger in a fast amount of time from a courteous staff. Within two minutes I could judge whether or not they fulfilled their mission. That day they did.

Within the context of Christianity our mission is as simple as that. We have a Christly story, a message of Good News. When we do that within our four walls on a Sunday we call that Church. When we do it outside we call it Mission, whether it is done nearby or halfway around the world.

Jesus is absolutely clear that we are to love one another, to be forgiving, to provide tangible care to those who are hurting, and to have faith. Do that with the attitude of the Beatitudes (Matthew 5:3-12) and the example of Jesus washing his disciples' feet (John 13:2-15), add in Paul's spiritual fruits (Galatians 5:22-23), and we have a rather direct Mission Statement for what we do within our walls and beyond, for Church and Mission. To simplify it, we are to stand for what Jesus stood for. Figuring that out is Church. Doing it is Mission. As with McDonald's, within a short time people can judge whether or not we fulfill our mission.

Fulfilling our involvement in mission always strengthens the local church. At the risk of sounding crass, every church I have served had more people in the pews, more money in the offering plate, and more kids in the Sunday school when I left than before I arrived. This is a direct result of what happens when a church jumps head and heart first into mission. The deepening commitment that comes from mission involvement results from, or causes, a deepening faith. The best of our mission always blesses the best of Church.

Jesus did not start mission work, he inherited it. God had been a sending, missionary God almost from the beginning. Abraham had been happily enjoying life in ancient Iraq, a town called Ur, when God said, "Get thee to a far country" (Genesis 12:1). It is a nice parallel to Jesus' "go ye into all the world." Both were surprising challenges to people not used to crossing boundaries, changing routines, trying new cultures, opening vistas, charting new courses, or starting a world religion. Neither the Old Testament's Abraham nor the New

Testament's disciples knew much about the world beyond their front door, yet God ordered them out way beyond their comfort zone.

From that moment on our God was a missionary God, and any people organizing a religion around that God need to be a missionary people. As God's children it is in our DNA.

Abraham's deal with God, called the Covenant, is a spectacular, two way agreement, maybe three way, involving God, Abraham, and the nation that would arise from their union: Israel. The deal is simple, if not so easy. If Abraham submits to God's will, God will bless Abraham with an infinite family tree through which the whole world would be blessed. Genesis 12:3, "and all peoples on earth will be blessed through you," echoes John 3:16, "For God so loved the world." That thought was not new with Jesus; God was expressing a divine, universal love all the way back to Abraham.

It is fair to say that Abraham and the next several centuries of Jewish generations got consumed with nation building, preferably their own. With the passage of time the original intent of the covenant, to be a blessing to the whole world, gets lost in the shuffle of priorities. God, however, never loses that missionary zeal. That is why we have Jonah.

The Book of Jonah is not just a seemingly fanciful tale about a whale. Indeed, it may be the most revolutionary book in the Bible. Like Abraham before and the disciples after, Jonah was happy in his hometown, among his people, living a daily life entirely familiar, surrounded by everything he liked. Into Jonah's idyllic life stepped God with a demand that turned everything Jonah lived for upside down. God's summons to Abraham to "get thee to a far country" and Jesus' challenge to the disciples to "go ye into all the world" could sound like invitations to exciting adventures — and Abraham's adventure at least came with a generous promise. Jonah's invitation was not an adventure, and did not include a promise. It was much more "Mission Impossible," minus Tom Cruise.

God wanted Jonah to go to, yes, Iraq, the ancient Nineveh. The people of Nineveh were evil from top to bottom, God was fed up, and Jonah was to deliver the sternest threat: shape up, repent, clean up your nation, stop the nonsense, turn to God, or else be destroyed.

Jonah says, "No." He doesn't like Nineveh, Iraq, can't stand their people, despises their history and traditions. In fact, he can't understand God's concern for them, it seems misplaced, and a waste. Isn't God the God of Israel? Weren't the Israelites called out of Iraq, leaving that God forsaken place in the dust in order to start both a new people and a new religion?! No, Jonah will not go to Nineveh, and neither should God if God had any sense.

To show his total independence from God, and his indifference, Jonah takes a ship, leaving behind Israel and, he assumes, the God of Israel (Jonah 1:3). This already revolutionary Bible story accelerates the revolution when God pursues Jonah, theologically obliterating national borders. God pursues Jonah, and when Jonah is tossed overboard and swallowed by the whale, God pursues Jonah down deep into the sea.

This was at a time in history when the world was populated with gods, large and small. Each nation had their own, each tribe, each clan, each family. In Genesis, Jacob and his wives decide to leave his in-laws' territory to return to Jacob's hometown. Fearing spiritual alienation his wives steal their "household gods," hoping that their divinity might make the trip. Such a thing was not done in those days (Genesis 31:26-34). Gods didn't make trips across boundaries.

Surprisingly, Jonah's God does make the trip, off land, out into the Mediterranean, down into the deep. Not surprisingly, Jonah has a change of heart, sees the light, agrees to go to Nineveh where, amazingly, he succeeds. Much to his chagrin, the hated Iraqi Ninevites repent, turn to God, all is forgiven, oh happy day.

But not for Jonah. The story ends with Jonah, moping under a tree, bitterly whining about God's love for all the world, that same love expressed in John 3:16.

This is hundreds of years before Christ, and already Judaism had a book in its scriptures that expressed God's determination that Good News, salvation, forgiveness, grace, and all the good stuff that comes later with Christianity, are meant for the *whole* world. The God who called Abraham out of Iraq to start a new religion sent Jonah on a mission back into Iraq to save their souls. Despite our separation through the years, there is in fact a seamlessness and unity to God's love as expressed throughout our shared Judeo-Christian faith.

The Biblical evidence for mission is overwhelming. God comes and goes and sends, and expects no less from us. The clincher, of course, is Jesus. My theological understanding of Jesus is that Jesus was similar to Abraham, Jonah and the Disciples. He, too, was content in his daily life up in heaven, comfortable in his celestial surroundings, enjoying the routine. Into that heavenly peace steps God with a shocking two-point charge. Jesus not only had to save the world, he had to go there, himself, in person. This "incarnation" interrupts Jesus' status quo and puts him squarely in our midst. Jesus was sent to us with a mission.

He was to leave the comforts and privilege of heaven to live humbly on earth. Once again, God is a sending God. Once again, a missionary is asked to do the impossible. As recounted in Philippians 2:5-8, "Christ Jesus, being in very nature God, made himself nothing, being made in human likeness. He humbled himself and became obedient to death on a cross." Jesus was a missionary.

To its credit, Christianity was the first religion to fully grasp the universality of spiritual truth. Other religions may have felt that they had the corner on truth but felt under no compulsion to share it. Religion was most often identified with a people, a place, a nation, a tribe, each identity group content to live its own truth. But Jonah and Jesus represent a God with a passion for everyone.

With the advent of Christianity, the critical question was, and is, how to share the Gospel Good News of God's love in Jesus Christ with people who already have a system of belief? Can it be done without hurt, without war, without threat? Sadly, Christians have been violent even toward one another, seeing every other Christian group as ripe for plucking, not as brothers and sisters in Christ. No wonder the Church has failed to be fully the expression of God's love in our going "from Jerusalem to Judea to Samaria to the ends of the earth." Jesus began his teaching with "love one another" before advancing to "love your enemies." We cannot do one without the other. And if we do one, we do the other. Until we do both our mission is imperfect.

I assume that in the world of mathematics there must have been a time when practitioners of math began to engage people with little or no rudimentary knowledge of math. As they did so, as they brought to light multiplication tables and advanced geometrics along with two plus two, did they do it without confrontation or hostility, without domination or division, other than long? Maybe math could teach Christianity a thing or two about mission. At its most basic, Christian faith is almost unique with its story of sacrificial love, universal love, and unconditional love. We should look like it.

However imperfectly, Christianity swept through the world like a tsunami, riding the waves of new convert enthusiasm, building on the sacrifices of martyrdom, powered by the basic truths of God's love. I use the image of tsunami deliberately. In 2004 a tsunami devastated much of South Asia, striking India's coast last, but no less ferociously. A church family on Christmas vacation contacted me immediately and sent a generous check for FOCI to help where we could. Alida took a team to the coastal fishing villages, distributing food, supplies, fishing nets to help the families restart their lives. I went further south, to mission work along the coast of old Madras, now renamed Chennai. We were not far from the martyred bones of St. Thomas, who was killed bringing the Good News to South India two thousand years before.

My host, a vibrant Indian mission leader, led me through homes and villages and churches that only days before had been full of life. Now they were thoroughly cleansed, no proof of life anywhere. The waves had come in, swept up everything and everyone, and then carried it all out to sea.

The tsunami was both cleansing and destructive. We cannot let the message of Christ's mission be a tsunami in the latter sense, hiding behind the false promise that after everything is swept away it will be clean. The people will remember the destruction.

Furthermore, our endless divisions and internal hostilities muddled our message as we competed for souls. My missionary hero, David Livingstone, could not keep himself from advocating for the three Cs: Christianity, Commerce, Civilization. We made sure the natives understood God's love, covered their breasts, abandoned drums, accepted our capitalism, forfeited lands, changed their names, learned our hymns, adopted our politics. Most of that has nothing to do with God's love through Christ.

The mistakes of our past should lead us to humility and repentance, not serve as an excuse to abandon mission entirely. Mission is not an option, or an extracurricular activity. Mission is the curriculum, it is the most practical proof of the oneness of God, the universality of God's love. In Church we teach it, study it, learn it, memorize it, plot it, plan it, advertise it, celebrate it. In mission we do it.

My sport is baseball, a sport that rewards a surprisingly low level of success. In baseball you are a star if your batting average is .300. That number represents a 30% success rate of hitting the ball effectively enough to reach a base safely. It therefore assumes a 70% failure rate. Usually that is high enough to discourage anyone from doing anything. However, in baseball the rewards of the 30% overcome the discouragement of the 70%. You may strike out in the first and fourth innings, but getting a double in the seventh inning will make it all worthwhile. Furthermore, if you struck out on a curveball you will practice harder against curveballs, hoping to get a hit the next time, all the while still facing odds against success.

Mission has struck out plenty of times. Poor leadership, narrow vision, inadequate resources, ego, vanity, personal failures have blinded us just as the curveball has broken into the strike zone. Time and again we swung and missed.

To end the analogy, we cannot let our failure rate predict or dictate our success rate. Perhaps we failed in the 1400s, and were too colonialist in the 1800s. Maybe we faltered in the 1900s. But we have been practicing, and whatever curve balls are thrown our way in the 21st century, we can be ready.

My journey in mission has taken me from the old days and old ways to the very real possibility of new days thanks to new ways.

This is not an exaggeration: I knew nothing about mission until 1974. I never heard about mission, studied mission, or met a missionary, an embarrassing admission. My lofty ambition to save the Church and change the world boiled down to being relevant on the one hand and political on the other, using Jesus as a pretext for both. I was busy enlivening deadly worship, counseling draft dodgers, chasing down runaways, ending the Vietnam War. That was as far as my eye could see.

One day in 1974 I opened up the New York Times, got to the Op-Ed page and read an article by Jeffrey Hodes that shook me to the core. He described a hellacious famine in sub-Saharan Africa that was destroying millions of lives and no one seemed to care. Given the high opinion I had of myself and my generation this was an insult. How could something so horrific be happening on such a grand scale and I not know about it? And the world not do anything?

In what now seems like a dizzying pilgrimage I ended up immersed in the world of mission. The famine article led me to a United Nations Church conference on famine and apartheid, which led to a mission trip to Africa with my American Baptist denomination, which led me to nine years as President of Habitat for Humanity International, which led me to doctoral studies in mission, which led me to India, which led me to found Friends of Christ in India (FOCI), which energized the churches I have served, which led to mission being at the heart of our church life.

Today I cannot imagine a healthy church in which mission is just an afterthought. It does not have to be exotic, it does not have to be overseas, but it does have to be the doing of the Gospel beyond the doors of your Sunday worship. Church worship is practicing hitting the curve ball. Mission is hitting the curve ball.

We cannot overstate the challenges of world mission in the 21st century and beyond. The last two thousand years we had a kind of wonderful naïveté that allowed some of us to head to the ends of the earth no matter the risks, and the rest of us to cheer them on. We celebrated as heroes and martyrs those who went to foreign mission fields and gave their lives. And while there were great risks, and many did suffer, the world in general was not officially closed. Our sense of adventure was often met by curiosity, and together we sought advantage, each from the other. The clash of civilizations was romanticized, even worthily so.

As I first headed into foreign missions in the mid-1970s I met a lovely, older, experienced missionary couple. They were gentle, humorous, quite unassuming, and thoroughly delighted to continue their life's mission in Zaire. It turned out that in what were euphemistically called "the years of chaos" after Zaire gained independence from Belgium, the missionary wife had been brutally gang raped by rebels before all missionaries were withdrawn. When the smoke cleared they went back, not defiantly, not wearing their outrage as a "red badge of courage," not trumpeting their ordeal and resilience. There was work still to do, they were missionaries, and that was their mission.

Later, in Zaire, I was befriended by two dear English ladies. They, too, had barely escaped from a rebel massacre targeting "whites" in general, missionaries in particular. Against all common sense they were leaving Kinshasa the next day to go back to the war zone. At a farewell prayer service the two ladies, in their 60s, were asked why they were doing it. They were the epitome of beatific as they answered in word and song,

When I survey the wondrous cross
on which the prince of glory died...

Love so amazing, so divine,
demands my soul, my life, my all. [25]

Jump ahead a few decades to today's world. Large swaths of humanity, easily half of the world, are ruled by governments which are openly hostile to Christian mission. From ISIS beheadings to visa denials, from restrictions on funds to restrictions on people, from treating Christianity as illegal to demonizing it, from persecution to murder, mission is under attack.

The answer is not to retreat. From the admitted safety of Greenfield Hill I imagine a generation ahead, or a century, or perhaps an age ahead, of martyrs from within and without. We have it already, whether intentional or unintentional. Jim Foley, the devout Catholic journalist, was the first world wide propaganda beheading for ISIS. The Egyptian Coptic Christians and the Ethiopian Christians were all executed for their faith in Christ. The Christian migrants traversing the Mediterranean, thrown overboard by their fellow migrants, Muslims; the Christians in Pakistan and Nigeria who dare publicly to go to Church; the defiant Christians in China standing up to government thugs who desecrate the churches; South Korean Christians who have died trying to help in North Korea and Afghanistan, these and more are modern day martyrs for God's love.

We dare not underestimate the cost of fulfilling The Great Commission, because in this age it will be exacted. Yet we dare that cost because we trust in God's providence to create a greater good than even the world's worst evil.

---

[25] "When I Survey the Wondrous Cross," Hymn 177, Pilgrim Hymnal, Pilgrim Press, 1983

This is not a morbid call for martyrdom. Ours is a religion of life, started by a miraculous birth, energized by the resurrection, and lived fully for others in between. It is in that selflessness that our greatest love is realized. The very nature of mission is that it takes your eyes off of yourself, it raises your sights, it expands your field of vision. Naturally, that begins right outside your front door.

While in Lusaka, Zambia I read a book by an English missionary to Zambia. I lost the book, don't remember the author, and can find no Google evidence of it. But his awful confession has stayed with me. As a missionary he was responsible to his mission agency back in London. Reports, accounts, balance sheets were the mundane parts of his job, which he hated and always put off. Under pressure from the head office he determined to finish all his required paperwork that night, no matter what.

As the night wore on he heard loud knocking on the front door of his mission house. Not wanting to be interrupted, he ignored it in order to focus on his mission work at hand. Later, the knocking returned and continued intermittently, at first persistently, then lightly. Toward dawn he thought he heard scratching at the door.

With the dawn the missionary finished his mission reports to his mission agency about his mission work. That morning, when he opened his front door, a dead man lay on his doorstep. Evidence of his dying pounding and scratching were clear on the door and his hands.

Mission is as close as our front door. At Greenfield Hill Church we have dramatically expanded our world mission, with substantial commitments to mission far removed from our bucolic, dogwood, country setting. The end result is that we do even more in mission within eyesight, foot walk, or a quick drive from our front door.

Some of it is obvious. No one in America has to look far to find poverty, hunger, homelessness. Thankfully, the opportunities to meet such needs and to serve people are ample, varied, even convenient.

One very hot Saturday our church members were doing a Habitat for Humanity work day in Bridgeport. Sawing, hauling, lifting, pounding, sweating, all to give one family a chance to live in a decent home. During lunch a friend said to me, "I'm glad to do this, but it is really not my strength. But I know banking. I know finances. If anybody is in trouble, let me help." Ever since that day my friend has saved family after family from ruin by offering financial counsel. He is a compassionate, eager miracle-worker. He is a missionary, fulfilling a mission, using his unique gifts, being Good News, a living example of God's love.

An interesting challenge is how to enable the Church's mission to be different than social service. I avoided writing "merely social service" because when you are in need there is no "merely" when it comes to being helped. Whether it is the government or United Way or the National Guard or an atheist, if they help it counts. Church mission, however, has a distinct flavor of faith. What we do is ordained by, motivated by, in response to, in partnership with God. We are not in it for credit, God is not looking for credit, but all that we do is meant to reflect a larger universe, a bigger picture. Even Jesus advised, "Let your light so shine that people will see your good deeds and praise your God in heaven" (Matthew 5:16).

Mission is holistic, a word I have seen spelled both holistic and *wholistic*. Either way, God is part of the holy and of the whole. To be truly either one God is there, not hidden, not covered up, not a silent partner, not an embarrassment, but innately part of the holy whole.

181

In the early days of Habitat for Humanity, when five dollars was still a big contribution, someone offered us five thousand dollars if we would stop highlighting our Christian faith. We needed that money, and the hint that sidelining our faith might lead to even more money was alluring. After all, we were in the business of building houses with poor people. Folks needed us, some quite urgently. What was to be lost by quieting our faith? Did each workday need to begin with devotions? Must each homeowner be given a Bible? What if the $5,000 could become $500,000?

We thought about it. After all, the main attribute of temptation is that it is tempting. But so is faithfulness. The truth for us was that Habitat had grown from nothing to something quite quickly, we were clearly on a roll, people were drawn to us, it was working, something good was happening. We might even call it miraculous. In fact, we did. Why, then, would we unplug ourselves from our power source? By hearing God's call, accepting God's challenges, and following God's scriptures, we found our mission fulfilled and fulfilling.

There are non-faith ways to be good. Atheists sponsored an ad campaign during Christmas that promised, "You don't have to believe in God to do good." There is enough good that needs doing for all hands on deck, whether atheist, humanist, or non-faith based NGOs.

Like McDonald's, anyone can create a mission statement, proclaim clearly what they do, and do it. Church mission, however, is tied to God's love. In our doing of good we are pointing toward a source of goodness larger than the individual good we are doing. On the first Monday of each month our church feeds the poor and hungry and lonely at a "community dinner," an old fashioned soup kitchen. Fifty to eighty people receive a hot meal within the confines of a Church hall, served by teenagers and adults. Over time faces become familiar, stories are shared, people move from behind the counter to sit side by side, prayer is offered, good is done, our Church is thanked, nourishment is given. The evening is an overt expression of God's love, it is offered as worship. There is a mystical union among God, the server, and the served.

We see this most clearly in our Appalachia mission. Greenfield Hill Church is almost three hundred years old. If we are famous for anything it is our historicity that earned us an historical preservation grant to fix our roof; for our Dogwood trees that earned us our nickname as the Dogwood Church; for our long ago pastor, Timothy Dwight, who went on to fame as Yale's President; and for our simple beauty, and our old, white, wooden church nestled in a country setting that oozes peace.

Fame and impact are two different things. Appalachia is our impact. Forty years ago we sent a station wagon of teens and parents to work with Appalachia Service Project (ASP), a teen-based Christian mission that uses home repairs as a way to teach the realities of God's love. Our ASP trip has grown to more than two hundred each year, broken into work crews of five teens and two adults each. Twelve-hour bus rides into the mountains and hollers of forgotten, poverty-stricken America in Appalachia result in an unmistakable miracle. The mystical union I observed in Calcutta takes place each week in filthy, sweaty work crews in Appalachia.

The people we send are not holy men and women. They are teenagers consumed with sports, technology, hormones, and college applications. The adults are business people with lives controlled by commuting, travel, the economy and competition. Yet buried in dirt, dodging spiders, carrying cement, sawing boards, roofing and plastering, day by day they are immersed in the eucharist.

That is heady talk for a fun filled week of do-goodism that is heavy on junk food, fireworks, and summer break. Yet I call it eucharist, which, after all, means "thanksgiving." Mission is thanksgiving.

Clichés become clichés because they are true. One cliché is spoken by everyone who ever does good deeds for others: "I got a lot more out of it than I gave ... this did a lot more for me than it did for them." Jesus no doubt knew this would happen when he issued his Great Commission. Throughout the Gospels he urges us to go into all the world, to pick up our cross and follow him, to love others as we love ourselves. Jesus knew from the beginning that the good we do through our mission would rebound to us as a blessing. It is the endless circle of love, that whatever love we give returns to us as love. That is not the motive for mission, but it is the fact of mission.

Nearing the end of his earthly life, trying feverishly to prepare his disciples to carry on the mission, Jesus gave what some call "The Final Exam," Matthew 25:31-46. He celebrates one group for what they did do for others, and castigates the other group for what they failed to do. In a fascinating twist, what we do for the hungry and thirsty and lonely and any in need is celebrated as being done personally for Jesus; and what we do personally for Jesus is rewarded with "the Kingdom prepared for you since the creation of the world" (Matthew 25:34). God's plan all along was for us to live love so fully that we would love our way all the way back to paradise. Now I know why every time I return from some mission experience I say, "that was a slice of heaven."

TEN

I Kissed the Feet of Jesus

I kissed the feet of Jesus. It was the most powerful worship experience of my life. Unexpected, so very far from my own world, way out of my comfort zone, but it was the fulfillment of every bit of my heart's desire when it comes to worship.

In 1990 I went to Guatemala City for a Habitat retreat of our Latin America staff. Still a runner in those days, I got up early on Sunday to run the streets, a great way to get to know a city from the ground up. On the run I saw crowds gathering on the plaza in front of the great cathedral, and I decided to return after showering.

In those days I was quite put off by the ornate wealth of Catholic Churches in Latin America. Gold and silver everywhere, expensive tapestries and priceless art, resplendent high altar and well-vested clergy. Over time I have grown to appreciate such churches a bit more, seeing them as being like a sacred trust. However, the contrast between the poverty outside and the wealth inside is jarring. I did not enter the cathedral expecting anything. I did not think there was anything for me.

God thought otherwise.

If the purpose of worship is to know God, and I believe it is, I was about to be encountered.

Sidebar. While auditing courses in World Religions at Harvard, I learned that one goal of Hindu worship is "darshan," to see and to be seen by the god or goddess at a particular temple. When you enter a temple you ring a bell to announce your presence. You stand before the idol of your choice, offering your worship.

Judeo-Christian religion may oppose idols, and yet we make room for tangible expressions of God. The Ten Commandments can forbid "making yourself an idol in the form of anything" (Exodus 20:4), but we humans yearn for something to feed our imagination, something expressive or representational. Something visual. Even with Exodus 20:4 as background, we Christians skirt the issue with stained glass, sculptures, saints, and relics.

The same Bible that warns against idols and graven images also says, "I love the house where you live, O Lord" (Psalm 26:8) ... "one thing I ask, that I may dwell in the house of the Lord all my days, to gaze upon the beauty of the Lord and to seek him in his temple" (Psalm 27:4). We want to "worship the Lord in the beauty/splendor of his holiness" (1 Chronicles 16:29).

In short, we want "darshan," we want to know God, we want God to notice us, we want the kind of encounter I had in the Cathedral of Guatemala City.

Entering this Roman Catholic, Latin American cathedral grand in scale, packed with people, and rich in ornamentation, I stood in the back as a dispassionate observer. This deserves another sidebar. The more I have been exposed to world religions the more challenged I have been, in Harvard's Diana Eck's words, to see the sacred in their worship. No matter how strange it may seem, or unfamiliar, or uncomfortable, or different, there is always a common denominator. Someone is trying to connect with God. Strip away questions about theology, doctrine, practice. Skip over matters of taste, style, or preference. Someone is trying to connect with God.

It took me a long time to learn that. I was more likely to stand back, a bit judgmental, a bit of a spectator, too theologically cautious to try to find God in some unusual setting.

One Sunday I was preaching in Haiti. Midway through the service a large contingent of white Americans arrived, and were given the most prominent seats. When it was time for Holy Communion the pastor of the Americans dramatically waved away the Haitian Deacons who were trying to serve his group communion. The American pastor did not want his people drinking wine. When the Haitians explained that they were using grape juice, he even more dramatically waved the Haitians back to serve his people.

Religious people spend a lot of energy waving off the religious experience of others. I have certainly wavered at Hindu Temples, mosques, Pentecostal churches, voodoo huts, Buddhist shrines, Reverend Moon's mass weddings and a Jerry Falwell revival service.

In each of those experiences I stood off at the side, literally and figuratively, striking the pose of interested bystander, bemused tourist, observant anthropologist, enlightened critic.

I was about to wave off the worship at the Cathedral of Guatemala City when suddenly I saw something that intrigued me. Off to the side was a life size statue of Jesus on the cross, a sculpture, really. A line of people was waiting patiently for the opportunity to come before the cross, climb up on a pedestal before it, and offer their personal devotion. Most people said a little prayer, softly or silently, then reached out and touched Jesus' leg, caressing it, before leaning in and kissing his feet.

Why was I intrigued? What struck me? The contrast between the formal goings on in the main part of the sanctuary compared to the simple piety of the people before the cross? The literal touchy-feely aspect of that piety? The intensity of their emotion, so visible in their eyes, their faces, their whole bodies as they embraced Jesus? The sense that this was real, I mean really real? Up on the main altar the Cardinal and priests were turning the water and wine into the really real body and blood of Jesus. Could not the intense devotion of these believers have the same effect upon a sculpture, a transubstantiation from art to life?

Well, I got in the line. As the line moved and I got closer to Jesus on the cross, I grew uncomfortable. I got out of the line. Twice. This whole scene was very un-Protestant, un-Swedish, un-New England, un-me. But even out of the line I could not take my eyes off of the sculpture.

I have not done justice to this sculpture, this thing, this crucifix. The cross itself was about six feet tall. Jesus, nailed to the cross, was about my height, five foot six inches. The body was what you would expect from medieval Catholic art with a Latin American aesthetic. It was garish, bloody, graphic, painful to behold. The wound in his side, the nails and holes in his feet, the blood dripping down his face from the crown of thorns, it seemed surreal. Yet more than that, the honest truth is that it was so real.

Well, I got back in line. Soon it was my turn, and it seemed too late and too embarrassing to back out a third time. Quickly, furtively, I looked around over both shoulders, as if to be certain that nobody would recognize me. The man behind me nudged me along.

Finally, I climbed up on the pedestal. I said my prayer. I reached out my right arm and began to stroke the leg of Jesus, as if I could take some of the pain away. Then I leaned forward and kissed Jesus' feet.

It was the single most profound spiritual experience of my life.

Catholic worship highlights the "mystery of the Mass" whereby Jesus becomes present in the Church. The wafer, whose nature is transubstantiated into Christ's flesh, is even referred to as the Host. Mother Teresa, in her writing, tells of waiting longingly each day for Mass when she could be with her beloved, her betrothed, Jesus. It is that personal, that real. In evangelical Protestant churches the preachers demand to know if you have a personal relationship with Jesus Christ.

Over at the side of that Guatemalan cathedral I had a personal relationship with Jesus Christ. By some mystery or miracle the substance of what I touched changed into something quite different from simple wood or religious art. I had my "darshan."

The idea of Church, the hope of Church, is to be a place to know God. When we do that it is good Church. When we don't, it is bad church, a waste of time and space.

One Holy Week, the day before Easter, I received this email:

> Reverend Rowe,
>
> I would like to encourage you this Easter Sunday to boldly proclaim the meaning behind the death and resurrection of Jesus. It is this message that is so vital for people to hear, the message of salvation and redemption from sin. As an eight generation direct descendant of the first ordained minister of the Greenfield Hill Congregational Church and a true Christian, I would like to thank you for you and your wife's service in spreading the Gospel. Happy Easter and God bless you!

To be honest, Alida and I smiled at first at the thought that we would need reminding to preach the Resurrection on Easter — it is, after all, the central point! Just as quickly, however, we realized it was a friendly email, quite affirming, reminding us to remember that what we believe is, above all, <u>Good</u> News. Naturally, if you love your Church and love your people you will love every chance to present and represent Good News. Sometimes, most times, Church is that simple.

Let's face it, anything that is still around after two thousand years is bound to be layered over with complexities of every kind: structural, theological, liturgical, and organizational. The challenge, even the privilege, of each generation is to simplify those complexities. I am not opposed to many of the new trends in Christianity, some I even admire. However, I have chosen a style of Church life that hearkens back to simpler times.

It took almost fifty years of preaching to finally stumble into the "perfect sermon," and it, too, was surprisingly simple. To say "perfect sermon" doesn't mean it was "perfect" in delivery or execution. But it is perfect in getting at the absolute heart of Christianity, perfect in reflection on the life and teaching of Jesus, perfect in relevance and application, perfect in scripture. Above all, it is perfect Church.

A sermon, like Church, is rooted in scripture, and this perfect scripture for perfect Church is Mark 2:1-12. Jesus arrives at a village and is inundated with people who want to see him, hear him, meet him. Meanwhile, across town there is a group of guys with a friend who is paralyzed. Their whole lives they had watched their buddy struggle to survive, a life consigned to begging and pity.

Hoping for who knows what, they determined to carry this friend to Jesus, only to find the house packed, every entrance blocked. This doubled their resolve. They climbed onto the roof, removed tiles or thatch, created quite a scene, opening a hole large enough to lower their friend at Jesus' feet.

In short order Jesus gives what I call "The Good News" and "The Better News." He tells the paralyzed man, "Your sins are forgiven ... rise up, and walk" (Mark 2:5, 11). Some in the crowd were shocked by Jesus' audacity in forgiving sins, but he was laying the groundwork for an even greater miracle. Jesus was doing first what only he could do: forgive. That is the divine part of this story, the Good News. The human part of the story is Jesus challenging the human, the paralytic, to grab ahold of life, to live to his potential, to take God's miracle and build on to it the miracle of his own life. His sins are forgiven, all well and good. Now comes the "better news," if he so chooses, to "rise up, and walk."

Jesus' invitation is a strongly implied sermon to all of us. Get up off your duff. Forget the past. God has a purpose for you. You have a purpose. The world needs you. No more lying about. No more excuses. No more watching life go by. "Rise up and walk." Get out of the house. Get moving. Get doing. Get living. Get loving. Jesus' "Good News/Better News" challenges us to decide who we are, what we are made of, where we are going.

Church exists to accomplish both, to assure forgiveness and to empower movement.

To proclaim boldly that we are forgiven is a joyous privilege almost beyond compare. The whole world is saddled with sin, even if we don't call it that. Some call it regrets, or the past, or failures, or memories, or injustice. To some degree or another we have done unto others what we would not want done unto us; and we have badly, unfairly been done unto. Personally, nationally, culturally, the whole world is saddled with sin.

A better mind than mine has said, "Forgiveness is the act of giving up my right to hurt you for hurting me." Such thinking is a rare combination of generosity and humility, recognizing the depth of one's own hurt received, and the likelihood of one's own hurt inflicted.

It is stunningly Good News that all of that is forgiven. Think of the paralysis in the Middle East, in broken relationships, in personal behaviors, among religions or neighbors, in families or communities. All of it is rooted in some perceived sin by one side or the other, and usually both. To all who are paralyzed, to a world of paralysis, Jesus starts with Good News. You, they, we are forgiven.

What Jesus guarantees with his death on the cross he proclaims to all who are paralyzed by sin, failure, brokenness, and disappointment. "Rise up and walk" is Jesus' statement of faith in the paralytic and in us, daring us to fully live the life that awaits us, unburdened by any past.

The Church has done a good job delivering the Good News, although too often packaged with the Bad News of condemnation disconnected from Jesus' priorities. I have yet to hear one sermon that promised hell-fire for not feeding the hungry. But I've heard and read many a sermon connecting damnation with homosexuality, communism, masturbation, Obama, and alcohol.

Yet by and large the world knows that Jesus died on the cross, and that somehow our sins are forgiven because of him. From old-fashioned revivals to modern day satellite televangelism, from little country churches to mega churches, from the old "Four Spiritual Laws" handouts to personal witnessing, from Gospel Music to mass media blitzes, from missionaries to the astounding statements of the victims' families in Charleston, the word is out: you are forgiven.

Then what? What is the next step?

The people of "Mother Emanuel" AME Church in Charleston epitomize the power of Jesus' bold declaration to "rise up and walk." On June 17, 2015, at the conclusion of a Bible Study open to all, a hate-filled terrorist murdered nine people. In the annals of American history that date may rival all others, including 9/11, for the transformative power unleashed across America. For a hundred and fifty years the truth of the Confederacy, the purpose of the Civil War, the meaning of the Confederate flag flying on State Capitols had been camouflaged by the nostalgia of "Gone with the Wind." Rhett and Scarlett had won the public relations battle. Symbols and vestiges of racism were left standing, from black lawn jockeys in the north to Confederate flags in the south to watermelon cartoons on the Internet.

Racism, America's "original sin" as many have pointed out, stood strong against all the hopes engendered and progress made from the days of Martin Luther King, Jr., the Civil Rights Movement, and the post-racial hopes for the Obama presidency. The Confederate flags kept flying and the lawn jockeys kept smiling.

Yet within hours of the Emanuel murders, America began to rise up and walk. When the murderer was arraigned the victims' families stood united in the courtroom and boldly proclaimed the Christian Gospel. The murderer was unmoving, paralyzed by his hatred and fear. One by one those families echoed Jesus' words of miracle, telling him that he was forgiven, inviting him to repentance and salvation, offering him the opportunity to get up off his mat of self-pitying, neighbor-hating paralysis, and to walk like a real child of God. What's more, the response of the families and of Emanuel's congregation and of the wider Charleston community was rooted in Jesus' Good News. They were quoting him, emulating and echoing him. Better yet, they were living his Good News, and modeling the way forward, for America as well as for the murderer.

Within hours sacred symbols of racism were being questioned not from a holier than thou, finger wagging distance but from within. Traditions, explanations, excuses, blind spots, ignorance, and history were challenged, discussed, refuted. Flags came down. Maybe a lawn jockey got retired. Hatred was seen as hatred, not humor or "freedom of expression."

The horrible slaughter at a Church Bible Study exposed the wounds we had long denied.

Wounds may be the salvation of the Church. I first began to wonder about that after kissing the feet of Jesus in that Guatemalan cathedral. It is true that rubbing my hand along the legs of Jesus was electric. In healing there are certain methods of drawing a poison, an infection, a parasite out of a hurting body. In that cathedral some of the worshippers could not leave the wounded Christ without trying to take away some of his pain. This is not a guess, it was that obvious. It was the truest worship of my life, the holiest experience of Church.

Tomás Halík took my long-ago wonder about healing wounds and gave it scriptural theology. For Halík, it is the wounds of Christ that give Church its power and purpose, and hope. And it is people like Halík who give me hope.

I have been blessed to have a mentor-type figure at every stage of my life. Indeed, I would bet that the key to a blessed life is to have a series of such people spaced across one's life. For me some came and went, some were around a long time, some ended badly, some I am just getting to know.

An irascible baseball coach, a profane and demanding English teacher, a saintly Old Testament professor all left their mark. Millard Fuller, founder of Habitat for Humanity, left more scars on me than impact. But the truth is that for a decade his teaching and preaching and, above all, his bold vision shaped my life. Two legends in world mission, Orlando Costas and Jonathan Bonk, always presented Christ with arms outstretched beyond anyone else's imagination, and they matched him. Key friends emerged at just the right time. Each epoch, each era, each decade brought the right person into my life.

Tomás Halík, the Czech priest I mentioned in Chapter 4, may be the least likely and the most providential. Coming at this stage of my life and career, his unbridled enthusiasm for the Church is a fresh tonic.

On my first visit to Prague I was expecting to find a dormant, even dead, Christianity. My first Sunday morning in Prague seemed to confirm it. Early that morning I crossed the picturesque Charles Bridge, climbed the steep cobblestone streets to the Castle, and entered the magnificent St. Vitus Cathedral, with the Cardinal presiding. It was the Mass of the day at the national cathedral of the Czech Republic, but there were only about thirty of us in attendance. After Mass I tried to tour the cathedral, its historic tombs and art and brilliant stained glass. But we few worshippers were rushed out for the paying customers. The cathedral was about to open for the tourists.

My assumption of dead Christianity was shattered several hours later. Still overwhelmed by the beauty of Prague, I had taken another long walk across the river, up the hill, exploring the wonders of old central Europe. Returning to my hotel I had to cross the Charles Bridge, which ends at the front door of another Catholic Church. Something was happening there, a crowd spilling out onto the sidewalk. Doing my best imitation of a lost, somewhat eccentric, absent-minded professor with my ever-present tweed sports coat, I edged my way into the church. I was astonished and heartened to discover that every pew was packed for evening Mass, with many young adults in the congregation.

Eight years later, on another visit to Prague, this time with Alida, I took her to visit that same church on a Sunday night. We had just been talking about what I most hoped to accomplish on this trip: finding the author Tomás Halík. A few months earlier, *The New York Times* had published an article about Halík. The interview, the quotes, the 'back story', all intrigued me. I began a hunt for his books. I had paid a hefty price for one of his few books in English, *Patience With God*

(Halík's study of Zacchaeus), and it had been worth every penny. Halík's ability to take an ancient story, treat it faithfully as the Gospel, and use it to face one of the great challenges to Christianity, atheism, was breathtaking. I had found his books, now I wanted to find him: I *had* to meet Halík while I was on this trip to Prague. But my internet sleuthing skills failed me; I had not found a way to contact him.

As I explained all this to Alida, we pushed our way through the crowd and into St. Salvator Church Klementinum ... only to discover, to my astonishment, Tomás Halík preaching! This was the center of his "Academic Parish of Prague," ministering to the university community. It was his ministry that had, eight years earlier and again on this visit, filled an ancient church with life, energy, faith and people.

An hour later, back at the hotel, Alida scoured the church's website until she found Halík's email address. She sent a fan letter on my behalf begging for just a ten minute visit with him. Over the next week, we met at length, and I continued to worship at St. Salvator, always impressed by the depth of faith, optimism and commitment I saw around me.

Halík is of that post World War II generation that grew up behind the Iron Curtain of Communism. Communism was meant to be the Savior for countries that had been failed by democracy, Christianity, capitalism. The new Savior of Communism, literally Stalin, did not want the competition of the old Savior, Christ or Christ's Church. By the time Halík felt the undeniable urging of God to enter the ministry, the Church was under fire, literally and figuratively. Churches were closed or taken for other purposes. Clergy were imprisoned, or restricted. Religion was marginalized, opposed, rejected. One of Communism's most effective weapons was using a large segment of the population as informers against everyone else. The simple act of walking into a Church for Sunday worship was an act of courage, and risky. To become a priest was to become a marked man, an outcast, an "enemy of the people."

Halík became a priest, so deep underground that he was not able to tell his mother for twelve years. As Czechoslovakia (now the Czech Republic) undertook its twenty-year journey to freedom in fits and spurts it was an unusual team that led the surge: rock musicians, writers, Christians, and students.

Halík was in the mix. His friendships with Vaclav Havel, Mother Teresa, Pope John Paul II kept him focused on a faith, a Church and a worldview that dared to imagine a life beyond petty tyranny.

A life of sacrifice and faithfulness prepared him for dynamic ministry in the turbulent years before the Velvet Revolution set the nation firmly on its course toward freedom, and ever since.

Now I can read his books. Now I can see his Church packed. Young people come in droves to learn from him. The world honors him.

The World Church needs him.

Two hundred pages of a semi-memoir, with a mini-theology of Church, is ending with a plug for a Czech Catholic priest. Because he gets it.

Religion in general and Christianity in particular are beset by doom and gloom. Whether it is ISIS slaughtering the innocent or churches dwindling into obsolescence, the world of religion seems headed downhill with the Church as an irrelevant bystander.

It is invigorating and empowering, therefore, to be with someone whose idea of Church is magnificent. Halík is not alone. Early in the writing of this book I visited with a Baptist pastor friend in North Adams, Massachusetts. The Methodist Church across the street is now a contemporary art museum. Down the block is an empty Catholic Church for sale. Another local church is now an apartment house, while another was sold to a Nursery School. The local hospital had just closed, and storefronts were empty. Yet as I sat with my friend he was excited, determined, bubbling over with enthusiasm. "What a great place to be a pastor," he said, "and what a great time to be a Church."

That is a New England version of Halík. Halík looks at the wounds and scars all around and makes the same proclamation: what a great time and place to be Church.

He sets this optimism squarely in the Gospel. As we sat in an alcove off the main altar I felt like I was sitting with those long ago disciples around Pentecost, when every ounce of their being was infused with God's "can do" Spirit. The world and all its ills, all its negatives, all its obstacles held no power against faith, whether St. Thomas then or Father Tomás' now. For Halík the world is filled with Zacchaeuses, yearning secretly to know Jesus, and in the knowing to be forgiven. And the world is full of wounded, hurting, paralyzed people yearning to be called so that they, too, can rise up and walk, forgiven and whole.

Any Church that is offering those two great miracles, forgiveness and purpose, will never go out of business. The entire world is made up of people who are hungry, yearning, and seeking. Jesus' uniqueness was that he met people where they were, he did not wait for them to show up at his house, he didn't even bother to have a house.

Instead, Jesus comes to us, to where we are. Halík retold for me the lessons he drew from the story of Zacchaeus in Luke 19, emphasizing Jesus' determination to go to Zacchaeus' house. The wounds of Zacchaeus' life, those he inflicted and those he suffered, would be touched and transformed where lived, in his world.

Halík became even more animated as our visit moved to this issue of "wounds." As always rooted in scripture, he expounded on the fascinating account of Jesus confronting his "Doubting Thomas" (John 20:24-29).

Beginning with Easter morning Jesus had been convincingly encountering his friends, but the disciple Thomas was never present. Thomas' doubts grew at the same rate that the faith of his friends grew. His doubt was blunt and specific; he said, in essence, "Unless I can see the wounds in his hands, and put my hand in his wounded side, I will not believe" (John 20:25, paraphrased).

In effect, for Thomas the wounds were Jesus. No wounds, no Jesus. To hammer home this connection Halík told me a legendary story of St. Mark. One day in an effort to undermine the spread of Christianity, the devil came to St. Mark disguised as Jesus. Mark was astute enough to request of this apparition, "Show me your wounds." The devil had done his research for the most part; he had the robe, the sandals, the height, the overall appearance of Jesus correct. But the devil forgot the wounds. Mark knew he was a fake. No wounds, no Jesus.

This is the powerful truth of the Gospel, and Halík emphasized that the only times when Jesus is directly referred to as "God" are in the midst of his suffering. The Roman Centurion, having watched Jesus die, proclaimed, "Surely this man was the Son of God" (Matthew 27:54). He came close, but Doubting Thomas nailed it. When Jesus bared his wounded side and opened his wounded hands, a fully believing Thomas declared, "My Lord and my God" (John 20:28).

This is the astounding, paradoxical crux of Christianity. Our religion of love and life is launched by the stark reality of wounds. The side effects of death. Jesus' wounds were proof of love and proof of life.

Halík's Church for the 21st century embraces a worldwide view in which wounds are not off-putting, messy, or proof of weakness. Instead, as they were for Thomas, wounds are life affirming and faith calling. They get our attention, they move us to worship, they spur us to love.

Azariah, my Indian colleague, taught me two expressions that go hand in hand: "Christlikeness," and "See a need, meet a need." We are to be as much like Christ as possible, and the most visible proof of that is to be fully present in the wounds of the world. Azariah was not much for five-year plans or goal setting. In his world some wound was always present, and that person became his five-second plan, and his goal. You see the need, then meet it. That is a living Church.

The living Church will never be irrelevant, or go out of business. It, we, may change structures, formats, styles. Halík cautioned me that seekers are not dwellers. Today's Zacchaeuses may yearn to see Jesus, and may come to us for a while to make that connection/introduction. But they may not buy a pew as in old New England. Or become a Church trustee or Deacon, or chair the Church Fair.

My fear in closing this book with Halík's theology of wounds is that I may fail to express the utter joy of Halík's ministry, and Azariah's and the Fire Tender's, and Mother Teresa's, and ours at Greenfield Hill. A wounds theology can sound onerous, burdensome, overwhelming, daunting. Not in my experience.

So I close with a movie scene. The sermons I heard growing up, from childhood through chapel at prep school, college and seminary, were full of Bible, Reader's Digest stories, Peanuts cartoons and literary classics. Mine are filled with Bible, contemporary novels, my own personal stories, and movies. The power of film to interpret faith is a great gift.

In the film *Places in the Heart* Sally Fields plays a young widow trying heroically to hang on to her family farm. The film is filled with the violence of poverty, racism, meanness, injustice. Among the sorrows is the accidental shooting of Sally Field's movie husband, a policeman, by a black teenager. That youngster is killed by vigilantes, and the movie unfolds. People, good and bad, do their best and worst to one another. Love and hate vie for attention and supremacy.

In the end, and that is what Church is about, Love wins.

The movie has built to what seems like a nice ending before going to a whole other level. The closing scene takes place in a little country church not unlike ours. It is a little, white, plain, wooden box, where all the beauty comes from God and people.

It is Communion time in that little town church with its fractured, broken history. The communion trays, with tiny cups of grape juice and bite-size squares of white bread, are being passed from one worshipper to the next.

It takes a moment or two but then you realize: they are all there. The living and the dead, the killer and the killed, the outcast and the victor, white police officer and black teenager, they are all there, in the same little Church, together, enjoying Holy Communion.

That's not a Hollywood happy-sappy ending. That is faith straight from the Bible. The Old Testament's vision of the lion and the lamb nestled up to one another and the New Testament's declaration of a land with no more tears are the promises of our destination[26]. Church is where we live that faith along the way.

---

[26] Isaiah 11, Revelation 21

About the Author

David Johnson Rowe has had a career in ministry blending church, mission, and writing. While pastoring churches in New England and New York he has served as President of Habitat for Humanity, International and the Overseas Ministries Study Center. He also founded Friends of Christ in India (FOCI).

He is the author of *My Habitat for Humanity: The Mostly Good Old Days*, a theology of mission; *Faith at Work*, a theology of work; and *Fieldstones of Faith I* and *II*, poems based on scripture.